Solo to Sydney

F. C. CHICHESTER

Frontispiece

Solo to Sydney

by Francis Chichester

With a Foreword by Lady Chichester
and an Introduction by
The Baron von Zedlitz

CONWAY MARITIME PRESS
GREENWICH

*Dedication to the Baroness von Zedlitz
as a mark of great esteem*

First published 1930
This impression published in 1982 by
Conway Maritime Press Ltd,
2 Nelson Road, Greenwich,
London SE10 9JB

© 1982 Francis Chichester Ltd
ISBN 0 85177 254 4

Jacket photograph of Sir Francis Chichester
by Giles Chichester © Francis Chichester Ltd

Printed and bound in the United Kingdom
by Butler & Tanner Ltd, Frome

FOREWORD

"To a man with imagination a map is the key to adventure"

Solo to Sydney was given to me by Francis as a wedding present. We had met in Devon in 1936 and a week later he had asked me to marry him. I knew nothing of his flying life at that time, but Amy Johnson later told me, "You are going to marry the best navigator in the world".

Knowing nothing of those skills at the time, I realise now why I liked this book instinctively. There is a similar sense of purpose there which I came to recognise in the sailing life which I later shared with him.

His exuberance, enthusiasm and sense of urgency, combined with his tremendous attention to detail and infinite capacity for taking pains heightened Francis' satisfaction in having achieved something that had not been done before. But he did not learn easily. I have seen him patiently practising fly-fishing in a square in Chelsea – like Matisse, who said, "I have drawn this line a hundred times before I got it right".

Now fifty years later I still re-read this book with much pleasure. It is a good story of early pioneering, for as he makes his way across the world with optimistic faith and committment, he introduces some of the early aerodromes and aviators, those men who opened up the air routes of the world. No computers or monitoring for them. Since those days the world has become very small. Recently when I flew back from Australia in a big jet in twenty-four hours, it made his flight seem very 'period'. I was invited to the cockpit and saw the monitors and computers they had. Every minute we knew where we were – our height, speed, course, the wind, etc.

The whole book is compulsive reading, but I still find the flight through monsoons over Java and the later description of his entry into Australia the most vividly compelling. His forced landing at the water bore and losing his way bear witness to the fact that world mapping was very greatly needed at that time.

As Francis drew near to the end of his journey he began to dread the anti-climax of facing people and making speeches, which to him were more exhausting and depressing that the red dust storm which brought further hazard to his approach to Sydney. The familiar tension of the adventure was about to give way once more to the down-draft of life on the ground.

Sheila Chichester
London 1981

LIST OF ILLUSTRATIONS

INTRODUCTION

" IF one had been over the road before and knew the route and conditions . . . but then the Romance would be gone ! "

Romance is the key-note of this incredible flight. A novice airman, " The Fledgling " as " Mr. Punch " calls him, alone, in the smallest of planes, to the Antipodes. And, as Lindbergh said on a famous occasion : " This expedition was not organised for money-making purposes." An amateur in every sense, out for the thrill of an unexampled, unrepeatable experience; the " one-time joy " of the Greek philosopher. Read the chapters on the Arabian Desert and the crossing to Darwin and you will realise what Lawrence meant by the " tonic exhilaration of fear."

Chichester is a young man, 28, and has always been the same, since as an urchin he caught an adder and brought it home, in spite of bites; and survived. Ten years of varied and adventurous experience, completely on his own resources, were the real foundation of his achievement, rather than his extremely short aeronautical noviciate.

Cæsar, after adding Gaul to the empire, dictated notes from his diaries to serve as a guide for young officers, and his text book is still the best manual for the aspiring soldier. This book may serve in the same way as the manual of the aspiring airman; more than that, I should call his career a guide for younger sons; in a drab, over-civilised world, it shows that within the Empire, no special gifts but energy and determination may win the prize of swift adventurous success.

As a schoolboy at Marlborough, he was too original to shine; and at games he was handicapped by extremely short sight. Sheer determination won him his Rugby cap; but he left school early, and, obviously unfitted for sedentary life, was apprenticed to farming. An ineradicable propensity to race the farmer's horses brought this experiment to a disastrous end, and the ne'er-do-well was shipped steerage to New Zealand at eighteen. Three days later, an accident in the stoke hold gave him the chance of his first and most gruelling job as an emergency stoker. In New Zealand, he started work on a farm; found it dull, struck for higher wages; not getting them, cleared off to the King Country, then being broken in, and made good wages saw-milling and bush-felling. After six months he had saved enough to indulge the day-dream of his boyhood—authorship. Hiring a room in a small country township, he spent laborious days reading with the idea of self-education, and writing a novel, long since destroyed. In the evenings, he boxed or went for training horses with the lads of the village, to whom he explained himself as swatting for an exam. Presently, his savings petered out; it was less easy to get a job, and he wandered to the West Coast, where he spent a couple of years in coal mines and gold diggings. This period has left pleasant memories and a few firm friends. Mining appealed to a lad of 19 as a man's job, with a good dash of hard drinking and high gambling thrown in; but there was more than that: the West Coasters are held in New Zealand to be the world's kindliest and most warm-hearted folk.

But, much as he enjoyed this life and freely as he indulged in its cruder joys, Chichester had no idea of being a manual worker for long; when he had saved up £400 he went back to the North Island to try business. First as a salesman, partly to gain experience, partly for love of the variety and roving life. Selling the " Farmer's Register," he went from station to station in an old Ford, carrying his tent and tucker, and incidentally developing into a crack shot at rabbits. At this time chance brought him into contact with Mr. Geoffrey Goodwin, a young man just starting business and anxiously looking for the right partner, as regards character rather than capital. The combination proved remarkably successful; after six years of partnership, during which he had married, Chichester was in a position to carry out what had become the ruling ambition of his life, to become an airman. The firm of Goodwin and Chichester were pioneers of civil aviation in New Zealand; they had imported Avro Avians, and devoted much time and capital in the venturesome hope of ultimately developing commercial aviation. Chichester, besides wanting to learn flying, was anxious to re-visit England after ten years' absence, and to study commercial flying in America and Europe. The idea had already occurred to him that, if he could learn to fly, it would save shipping freight and be exciting fun to fly back.

Determination is a quality Chichester shares with many Englishmen; peculiarly his own is the capacity for taking infinite pains. Readers of this narrative will see for themselves that his mind works with intense activity, elaborating every detail, leaving him as exhausted as physical over-exertion; he always was a bad sleeper, and knows nothing of that empty passivity of heart and brain which most of us find so comfortable. Before leaving New Zealand he spent many a night hour thinking out details of equipment and training. He left New Zealand in April, 1929, with nine months before him. The trip opened disastrously: the strain of overwork and exacting business demands had knocked him out, and two months of the precious nine were lost in hospital at Los Angeles. His opening chapters give a detailed account of his training as an airman; instead of enlarging on that, I prefer to give you a memory that seems to me characteristic of the man. I was with him when he learned ski-ing in the Southern Alps; he took a long time, and surely no man ever had so many falls in a week. But he mastered the art sufficiently for his immediate purpose, which was to cover the long snow distances involved in winter mountaineering. He would make a first-class mountaineer. Time and weather conditions forbade an attempt on Mt. Cook; but with Oskar Coberger, a careful and daring guide, he scaled the face of Mt. Seely by an untried route, getting down somehow in the winter dusk by the ordinary ridge route, which is not safe or easy even in summer. He tells me that even now his usual aviator's nightmare of flying blind is occasionally diversified by a nightmare of ice-covered rotten rocks in a traverse or couloir.

He has been called " the world's shyest airman." One might add, the most modest. The other day I heard him make a perfectly characteristic remark talking to the Director of Air Services: " When Elijah is done up I shall go round New Zealand for a bit giving joy rides. . . . It's really the best way to learn to fly."

G. W. Z.

20th April, 1930.

CHAPTER I

THIS chapter, being an attempt to answer the question so often put to me : " How did you learn enough in five months to enable you to fly to Australia ? " should be passed over by anyone not interested in the a b c of learning how to fly.

Briefly, I only just did learn enough in the time.

It has been said that flying is an art, like writing or making love. If you can't do it nobody will ever teach you, and if you can nobody will ever stop you.

But about the art of flying there is at least one notable difference : the writer and lover can try and try again; the aviator must master his technique in the few weeks when the instructor is beside him to prevent a mistake from costing him his life. Let him set about correcting a nose-spin the wrong way when close to the ground, and he will be unable to explain to admiring younger sisters how even the art of flying must finally yield its secret to man's patience and force of will.

Personally, used to learning things off my own bat by the try and try again method, as, for instance, ski-ing, when I think I fell 444 times the first day, I found learning to fly with an instructor extraordinarily difficult, and in fact had to put in 24 hours' dual instruction before I was considered

13

safe to go solo five minutes. In the process I drove eight instructors to lifting the bowl of wine oftener than usual. " Land a plane," they'd say, " why! it's easy! " And so it is. It's as easy for a beginner as it is for a new-chum driver to steer his car through a six foot gateway, twenty consecutive times, at seventy miles an hour, without touching either side. And some young fellows who had just left school would be off solo after only six or seven hours dual. Sometimes I would despair. I'd make a perfect landing, but fifty feet above the aerodrome. More usually the instructor would save by inches the ship and crew, about to fly full tilt into the wire fence. Was I going to show myself a prize squarehead? Had I set my heart on doing the London-Sydney flight without possessing enough of the art to pilot a plane solo round an easy aerodrome, and in perfect weather? Here was I making a frightful fuss about that portion of the game which can be described as " Flying without tears." Why! that was nothing. I had to be back in N.Z. within six months from the day I landed in England, at the end of July. Here are some of the things I needed to become proficient at before I could think of attempting the flight :—

Cross-wind landings, right and left hand ditto, cross-wind take-offs, forced landings, heavy load landings and take-offs, night flying, compass navigation, sextant navigation, map-reading, sufficient mechanical knowledge to do any repairs necessary on my own engine, sufficient knowledge of rigging and repairing to enable me to execute at least rough repairs, drift-reading (which can be put in as a separate branch of navigation, it is so important in cross-country work), meteorology and

14

the handling of a plane under all the different weather conditions likely to be met with, the handling of Customs, police, military and civil authorities, the organisation of petrol, oil, and food supplies.

What equipment was best suited for the job? What happened if one struck, or were struck by, a monsoon or a waterspout? Here were all these problems waiting attention, while I yet despaired of reaching even that state of aeronautical bliss entitled " Solo."

And then, time was so short. When I left New Zealand I had intended to have six months for the job, but a severe operation which kept me in hospital at Hollywood, in California, until within two weeks of landing in Southampton, had shortened the available time by two precious months, besides leaving me, for my first month in England, still feeling pretty ill.

And when you are in a terrific hurry, what an exasperating business it is, learning to fly! To begin with, it was costing me £4 an hour for instruction. You might think the pain of paying £4 for sixty minutes in an aeroplane would be sufficient sacrifice to provide yourself with sixty minutes of unalloyed bliss. No, Sir, not a bit of it! Before you have finished your course, you will be seen with bended head, and hat in hand, humbly begging an instructor to allow you to present him with a trifling £4. The word " flying " you will not dare to mention. You will merely breathe a silent prayer that he will later call you out, put you in a plane, and tell you for half an hour a few of the worst of your crimes. Before you have finished, you will be so tamed, it will seem quite natural to wait all day at the aerodrome for a

15

lesson, to see half a dozen youths or girls pushed up ahead of you, and finally, at the end of the only fine day for a week, listen without remonstrance when told there will be no chance for you to have a lesson that day. Pay £4 an hour, why, you presently beg to be able to! But when is it possible? To-day it is calm and probably too bumpy. Another day it is not calm, and certainly too bumpy. This day the wind is in the wrong direction, another time it is too strong. To-day being Saturday, everybody has arrived for a lesson, and you are squeezed out. A fine day comes, everything is propitious; unfortunately the only machine left on the aerodrome has a split-pin in its intake manifold. On top of this, I found it useless to take more than half an hour's instruction any one day. If you do, your brain will get indigestion, and instead of advancing, you will be retarded. You quickly learn that it is a whole time occupation. You fancy you can neatly wedge in a morning's business, yet absorb the usual amount of aeronautical knowledge in the remainder of the day. Very likely the first result will be that you miss, by only a few feet, crashing into another kite when taxiing across the aerodrome. A few more narrow squeaks will prove that you are decidedly unsafe in a plane except when in the right mood. The get-rich-quick, go-getter, super-salesman mood is death and damnation in the air. Nowadays, I walk round and round my plane, fiddling with a nut here, or a control there, until that calm, benign and benevolent mood steals over me; such a mood as you feel must be the portion of some Ancient Mariner, when with a foot long ziff stirring gently to the sea breeze, and with feet crossed, he leans back against the dinghy's edge, pulling somnolently at his upturned clay, and with unwinking eyes contemplates the horizon.

However, learning to fly has its compensations. The day arrives when at last you make two 3-point landings in succession. It is the same as being in love: your heart swells with love for your neighbour, the drone of Cirrus engines no longer suggests incipient engine-knock at every beat, you forget your creditors, the world is at your feet, flying is child's play. It is incredible that you should ever have imagined it difficult. Your fancy flies ahead, you work out how you consider the controls should be moved for a slow roll or a half roll off the top of a loop; the intricacies of flying no longer hold any terrors. In short, complete happiness is your portion. Next morning you are up with the lark, and make a sorry imitation of him in your bath. You set out for the aerodrome with the nearest resemblance to a rush possible in London. Bursting with confidence, you board a plane. I reproduce some of the politer parts of the ensuing castigation:—

" Don't jerk your tail so suddenly, or one day in long grass you'll trip and nose over."

" Don't swivel all over the field. Watch a point on the horizon and take off straight."

" If you take off before you've got up flying speed, the slightest gust of wind will stall you, and you'll write off the undercarriage."

" The regulations are you must not turn till 500 yards beyond the aerodrome perimeter."

" You're turning with too much rudder, and not enough bank."

" Keep your nose down turning. Nose too high, too much bank, not enough rudder and side-slipping. You're asking for a spin."

17

" Watch your speed while turning. You'll lose flying speed and hit the deck before you can recover it."

" Make all your control movements smooth. You're jerking the kite about like a washing-machine."

" You are headed straight for that plane approaching. You must watch for other machines and keep to the right."

" The regulations for this aerodrome say left-hand circuits, so don't make them right-hand."

" Cut off your engine. Keep your eye all the time on the spot where you want to land. Widen your arc of approach as you are obviously over-shooting. Watch the flying speed on the turns. Try to keep the speed at a steady 60 miles per hour when landing. You have slight rudder on all the time and left wing is low. Give your engine a short burst, to see it's all right. You have flattened out much too soon. No use making a perfect landing 60 feet too high. Put on your engine and go round again."

Next time :—

" Man alive, can't you see you're headed straight for the fence? More engine quickly. Watch that plane taxiing across the aerodrome. He has no right to move while we are landing, but you can't run into him."

Bump! The wretched machine hits the ground and rebounds 15 feet into the air.

" For the love of Mike put on your engine when you do that, and don't wipe off your undercarriage by dropping back stalled on to the deck."

You then make the world's worst landing in a series of rabbit hops. The instructor (what a life!) inspects to see what damage is done. If

18

you are permitted to try another landing, the result will be much the same. At the end of the day, after the humiliating spectacle provided by a fellow student, who, with only a third of the instruction you have had, makes seven perfect landings in succession, you crawl humbly home, the sorriest dog in the world, unable adequately to conceal your tail between your legs.

CHAPTER II

AT last, on August 13th, the time really did come when I was pronounced more or less safe to pilot a bus solo, and I got in the first five minutes. From that time I was able to pick up things more rapidly. I set about acquiring an "A" or mug-pilot's license. First to put in seven hours solo. The only hardship in that was to translate it into £4 an hour. Then, on August 19th, the sealed barograph, to do the 6,500 feet height test. How important and dignified one feels as one climbs into the three-layered Sidcote suit necessary to stand the cold! At 7,000 feet I passed through a solid belt of cloud which totally concealed the earth from view. What a glorious, colossal snow field one travelled over! Not a break or change in it in any direction as far as the eye could see, just roll upon roll, wave upon wave of endless snow. Above, infinite space, illimitable emptiness, with only the sun shining brazenly, eternally. . . What complete isolation, solitariness! Such, I imagine, must be the sensations of a Polar flier. It was worth a lot to have that moment. But I desisted from climbing after reaching 10,500 feet, because by then I had had enough time to work out that it was costing 1/9 every extra 100 feet I climbed.

After the height test came the oral examination by the secretary of the Royal Aero Club. There are 150 articles of the Aeronautical faith to be mastered. It took hard cramming from 7.30 till

10 one night to do it. However, next morning I was able to satisfy my examiner on many abstruse questions, such as :—

" What arrangements of its lights enables one to distinguish a fixed balloon from a free balloon? What is signified by two white lights, vertically situated 6 feet apart and visible through a dihedral angle of 220 degrees? "   I wish I could remember. Fortunately in New Zealand sheep are more common than either fixed or free balloons. I must confess I would sooner run into a free sheep than any balloon, however lightly fixed.

Now approached the great moment !   I could fly a little, and was confident that I could learn to fly better. But navigation? Map-reading? Ah ! that might well be a different matter. Suppose I couldn't navigate across country?   Finding one's way about the bit of country I had seen while flying round the aerodrome had looked as easy to me as finding the missing link.

The first time I ventured away from the aerodrome was most exciting.   At first everything was a jumble.   Then I picked out a railway line, the Thames, Staines reservoir. With the aid of the map I found Byfleet. Flying at snail pace I recognised other landmarks shown on the map. Joy of joys ! If I could do that much the first day, competence must be a matter only of practice and experience. It was like beginning to swim : at first venturing only a few feet, then every day a little further.

On August 28th, I secured my license. On September 8th I bought a Gypsy Moth; it sounds simple, but was not so for me, because already my jam had been almost stopped owing to a slump we were having at home in New Zealand. Every

21

available scrap of paper not filled already with notes on how to fly and how not to fly, I filled with countless budgets on cost, maintenance, and (not least) expected repairs. I bought the Moth because I had taken a very strong liking to the Gypsy engine. It was not the plane I wanted. I had left New Zealand with the idea in my mind of buying a bigger and better machine. It was by now perfectly apparent that financial reasons made its acquisition impossible, so I bought what I could.

On the 11th I flew up to Liverpool, and thence on the 14th to visit my parents in North Devon. Here I learned Flying Lessons Nos. 17 and 18. I had been showing the lads of the village what a smart little boy I was with a real live aeroplane. On renewing my acquaintance with terra firma I made a shocking landing on a rabbit burrow. Thence bounding into the air I was overawed by a stately oak tree barring forward progress, so did not put on the engine. Bang! Down we came against the raised side of a concealed cart track. Like hoar frost on a window pane, burst the daylight through the side of the fusilage, and we came to rest with drooping plumage like a winged partridge. Well, that was no good to me. After ten years here was I back in the old home village. I could sense already how the air would vibrate with " I told 'ee so."

Short wave length, long wave length.

" There baint no good did ever coom fram they nu-fangled aireoplanes."

I scratched the old poll and then bethought me of Jarge Moore, who with his boxing abilities, became, in the days of my youth, responsible for the present plebian profile of my proboscis. At least, if he could break noses, he was a carpenter, and should now have a chance to mend compression struts. I rushed off pell-mell for Jarge, hoping no one would spot, meanwhile, the disembowelled flank of the plane. Jarge and I got busy with hammer and tongs.

"Fourteen inches of ¾in. by ½in." would say I. " Right " would say he. And in no time we had constructed soap-box replicas of the original struts, not to mention one or two additional ones we invented ourselves. Eighteen hours later we took to the air again. And a very nice repair too. F.L. 17 : Don't fly to impress an audience. F.L. 18 : Don't land in a cul-de-sac, whence you are unable to rise if you make a dud landing.

Next day I took our old gardener for a flight. He needed a mighty lot of persuading : in fact he is the only man I have ever pushed into coming as my passenger. But I thought it would be worth while to see the result, particularly as he had the breeze up so much beforehand. I had always had a warm spot for him (Wilkey was his name), since the day when, working in a quarry, he put his partner's best bowler on the blasting charge after the fuse had been lit. At the last moment he pointed out the hat to his partner. The owner of the hat nearly went mad with peeve. How I should have loved to see that bowler flying sky-high among a few hundred-weight of rocks big and small ! I understand the biggest rock, after describing a longer parabola than the hat, made a perfect 3-point landing fair and square on top of it.

When we landed again Wilkey said : " Do you realise what this date is, Master Francis? " " No," says I. " Well," he replies, " this is your birthday. Twenty-eight years ago this day 'twas I that was sent to fetch the doctor to help you make your first landing in this world. And I never did think that day, that 28 years later you'd be taking me up in an aeroplane."

Two days later, it being Monday, September 20th, the time arrived for me to set out once more for Brooklands. There was a pretty hefty breeze blowing, but with the help of Wilkey and my two sisters hanging on to the wings I taxied the old bus out all right. She seemed to rise vertically into the air, the wind was so strong. Thereupon I christened her Elijah, and Elijah she has been to me ever since. It is true that previous Elijahs have been of the male sex, but of course the best thing about every good rule is the breaking of it. My Elijah is a lady—a perfect lady.

Back we scudded at the rate of knots. No aeroplanes were out at any of the aerodromes we passed. It is a great feeling to ride the elements —provided you feel full of confidence. Inexperience sometimes accentuates this feeling, but never with justification, I fear. Even so I guessed landing would provide some fun, but I found the idea exhilarating. With this flight I had definitely passed the extreme novice stage, when flying is 3 per cent. fun and 97 per cent. wear, tear and fear, and exciting all the time. From now on it changed to 5 per cent. great exhilaration, 10 per cent. blue funk, 15 per cent. placid enjoyment, 40 per cent. slight worry, and the remaining 30 per cent. fatigue and tedium. At the same time there was still an undercurrent of excitement all the while. Of course, to get the 5 per cent. it is well worth putting up with the other 95 per cent., otherwise no one would fly.

It is good sport landing in a strong wind. As

24

you are a foot from the ground and just about to settle, a strong gust sends you up ten or fifteen feet into the air. When the gust dies down, you are left high and dry in a thoroughly stalled condition, whence you drop with a thump or your under-carriage, or prop. This will mean a ten days' sojourn in the rigging hospital with acute longer-onitis or propelleritis. If you put the engine on as the gust lifts, flying speed should be obtainable before the gust drops away again. I think one soon learns that the only way to land in a strong wind is to fly on to the ground and taxi in flying position with a little engine, until the machine has practically lost way, when it will need an excep-tionally hard blast of wind to lift it off the ground, provided always you keep going dead into wind.

My first shot at landing was a dud. I bumped, so went off again. Next time, although the kite kept on lifting from the deck, I flew it in carefully and came successfully to a halt. Fine! I felt proud of my piece of work. There is some proverb about pride. I began taxiing towards the hangars. This necessitated travelling across-wind. I had the interesting experience of seeing the port wing-tip dip slowly and gracefully to the ground. Unable to dip further, the tip slowly crumpled up. The other wing rose equally slowly till the whole machine balanced itself on the port wing-tip. Thence it seemed to take a leap into the air, landing fair and square on its nose, with the tail sticking up vertically towards heaven. I found myself in the undignified position of dangling in the safety belt and looking down at the ground ten feet below.

End of Flying Lesson No. 19.
Price £75.

I may say my rural repairs to the longeron and compression struts caused any amount of amusement to the riggers. They immediately wanted to know what colony I hailed from. Apparently it is not the custom in England for pilots to effect their own temporary repairs. At least these accidents were very valuable, in that I acquired elementary knowledge of repair work and rigging through them. Under the supervision of the chief rigger I worked for 50 hours during the next week, repairing the mess.

After this, I went solidly into training for the finer points of flying.

It seemed to me that the most important thing of all was the landing. I set about practising, to enable myself to land a plane safely—if not in pretty 3-point fashion—in the smallest possible space, no matter what the weather was like, no matter what the ground was like, no matter what mood one was in. Especially the last—to be able to land safely when unwilling to fly, too tired or not feeling fit. I used to fly when I felt least like it, testing each manœuvre almost to destruction; seeing how close to the fence I could land, how slowly I could bring Elijah in, with how much wind I could make cross-wind and down-wind landings. I used to stick a piece of cloth on the ground 150 yards from the fence, and practise by the hour, first touching the aerodrome where the rag lay, secondly finishing the run on top of the rag. In still air, the latter is extremely difficult to do with a Moth. You have to fly straight at the fence and at the last moment stall the plane over it.

In addition to the above I usually did half an hour a day practising forced landings. I used to climb to 1,000 feet and then, cutting off the engine, pick the best field I could. At first I used always to overshoot the field, because I entered so thoroughly into the game that I really thought my engine was now dead, and that to undershoot was fatal. After some practice one learns to make better approaches, so as just to skim the trees or fence surrounding the field picked. Judgment in estimating the size of fields is only acquired slowly. Nowadays I find it extraordinarily difficult to land in the middle of an aerodrome; I cannot get out of the habit of just hopping the fence however big the aerodrome may be. One often finds oneself scraping in at the extreme end of a big field, and then, after landing is finished, one takes off again to fly to the other end of the aerodrome.

The day's programme usually included half an hour's simple stunts, such things as loops, spins, and stall turns, to improve air work. One loop cost me £20. The locker lid came half open, and out dropped my best overcoat (also being my one and only), tool-kit, front seat cushion and hat. The hat was later found and caused much pleasure to the policeman who returned it. " I've returned many a lost harticle," he said, " but never yet hanythink dropped from a hareoplane." At the same time I had in the locker a pair of red and purple pyjama trousers. I used secretly to obtain much satisfaction by wearing these as a scarf. On landing, I discovered they had caught on the tail plane strut, and here they were flying fully extended in the slipstream of the propeller.

On October 4th my compass was installed and swung, and I introduced a little cross-country work into the day's programme. All the time I was checking up petrol consumption, speed, range, and errors in cross-country navigation.

27

Here is a day's entry in my log book about this time :—

" Oct. 10th. Ten consecutive left-hand landings within 30 yards of mark. Right-hand landings and circuits, loops, stall turns and spins. Cross-country to Sway, New Forest. Course of $263\frac{1}{2}°$ + 20° for wind drift. Accurate to Odiham, when course changed to 232° + 25° for wind drift. Flew above clouds for estimated time of 35 minutes, calculated to bring me out of clouds five miles short of objective. Came out at Lyndhurst $5\frac{1}{2}$ miles short of objective, and + $4\frac{1}{2}°$ off course. Time 65 miles in 1 hour 12 minutes, equals 54 miles per hour. Return course 64° — 30° for wind. Altered course to — 25° for wind at Southampton, proved — 6° too much still. Time 63 miles in 46 minutes, equals 82 miles per hour. Three landings over trees in twelve-acre field."

As far as actual flying was concerned, I began to feel more hopeful, except when I paused to think of what yet remained to be learnt. I never allowed myself to do that if I could help it, for fear of becoming depressed. At this point the cash dried up. My partner, G. D. M. Goodwin, and I conduct businesses in New Zealand, such as the selling of land, on the dollar-down-and-chase-one principle, the usual system there. Unfortunately a slump set in about the time I sailed for U.S.A. Our kind of business suffers most in a slump. The money is there all right, but can't be realised. It was unthinkable, the idea of giving up the flight at this stage. Some way of raising the wind would have to turn up. The first thing I did was to cut down expenses to an absolute minimum. For the first three months after leaving New Zealand, financially bumptious, I had done myself remarkably proudly at the best hotels in Los Angeles, New York and London, with everything in keeping, but now in pensive mood I was often to be seen reciting " To be, or not to be," before investing a penny in a penny-in-the-slot machine. That was the worst of my new acquaintances in London: I never could be the first in to borrow a match. The only things I never economised on were the petrol mixture of the plane, and the habit of frequently changing the engine oil.

Experience I was now gaining all the time. For instance, on October 5th I got temporarily lost in a storm over Exmoor, with a 75 mile gale blowing. I lost sight of the earth, which came into view again above my top plane; I was flying straight into a hill. On October 7th I took off in the dark from the field in Devonshire, but not without trepidation, because some pigs had evidently escaped and bent the tail elevators into a semi-circle, how I cannot imagine. I straightened them out as well as I could. These things don't worry you if you have experience, but without it you are unable to assess correctly the importance of any particular defect in an aeroplane. On October 14th I got caught by darkness 30 miles from the aerodrome, and safely faked a landing on top of a hill. I could not see the valleys; only the top of the hill, bald except for a flock of sheep collected on the top to sleep. My first swoop frightened the sheep and just enabled me to see there were no obstructions. The second circuit scared the sheep out of their wits and sent them galloping off the hill. The third time, now practically dark, I flew up close to the hill below the summit, flattened out

29

and settled on the top.

On October 15th I took off and landed in the moonlight at Brooklands. This provided me with 23 minutes of intense enjoyment, for the feeling of complete isolation and solitariness amounts to excitement. All those lights below representing millions of people who are as completely unable to help you or communicate with you as if you were living in the moon. I looped and did a few stall turns, for the same reason that a dog barks at something much bigger and stronger than itself. Then glided in as quickly as I could, unable to suppress the fear of law and order inculcated by years of motoring, which now caused me to expect the sight of the local P.C., notebook in hand, waiting to summons me for flying without lights.

On October 20th I went to a luncheon party at Birmingham. After dropping a passenger in a field near Witney, we got into a dirty storm on the outskirts of Birmingham. I imagined we should be across the town in no time. With the course we were following, there was so much drift to port that I had an unobstructed view of our track ahead. This enabled me to dodge the tall chimneys. There were so many of them that I dared not alter course to another direction which might not give me such a good view ahead. It was pelting with rain, and with the empty machine we were thrown about as if we were but an autumn leaf in a gale. Throttled down to 60 miles per hour, I thought we were never going to get through that town. Afterwards I found we had flown over 12 miles of practically solid buildings stretching to north of Wolverhampton. After fervently declaring nothing would shift me could I once reach terra firma safely, it is typical of flying that I should leave five minutes after landing in the first field I came across. Hundreds of people had swarmed out at me like ants. In addition the weather was foully wet, so I found out where I was and pushed off again. On the way home, dirty weather forced me to land in a field at Prince's Risborough, but I took off 20 minutes later. Here I learn F.L. No. 23: "Don't take off down wind in small fields." However, Elijah slotted over the hedge by the mud of her wheels. Next item was darkness, which caught me in the Chiltern Hills, rain and bumps being plentiful. I could see Brooklands was a bad proposition, so I shot for Northolt. I declared I would never get caught by darkness again, and wasn't for three days.

Time was now getting short. I saw I should have to forego much of the training in technique I was so keen to acquire. I put all my remaining cash into preparations for a trial spin round Europe. I determined to send a cable to Goodwin: "Do best to raise £400 necessary for swan song. Leaving for Europe." My intention was to rush round Europe, and then, if Goodwin could raise the wind, to start for home as soon as possible on return. If no money was forthcoming I should at least have bagged the fun of the European trip before the cash dog-fight began.

The first difficulty was insurance. As I still owed some money on the bus, I could not leave the country unless it were insured. Roumania is regarded as a bad insurance risk, furthermore my aeronautical status was that of mug pilot. Finally Captain Lamplugh underwrote the risk, provided I took with me Joe King, an experienced 'B' License pilot who had done a lot of aerial survey work in Bolivia.

31

SOLO TO SYDNEY

From the word 'go' on October 25th that trip was great sport.

"Let her go," says Joe King, pushing the throttle full open.

He being an experienced pilot, I assumed he wished to take the plane himself, so I dropped the controls altogether. We seemed a long time leaving the ground and then only just cleared the trees on St. George's Hill by a foot or two. However, I didn't bother, as that was in keeping with Joe's style.

"Hey!" roared a voice through the telephone, "what on earth are you doing?"

"Doing," I said indignantly, "why, I'm not touching any of the controls."

"Nor am I," says he.

However, they won't always take off by themselves.

At first Joe was a bit worried about me, and kept on asking whether I knew my bearings.

As it was my first Channel flight, I climbed to 6,000 feet in order to feel safe, and Joe asked bitterly if I wanted to turn him into an icicle. After a cognac or two at Abbeville, in France, his fears were sufficiently allayed to permit him to sleep soundly in the front cockpit during the rest of the afternoon. At Paris he found an old business friend. Not having seen her for a long time, there were such arrears of business correspondence to make up that he remained, and I carried on solo.

That trip was a great experience for me. In 25 days I visited eight countries. Of 28 landings, eight were in fields. Of these eight landings, three were for fun, two caused by fog, and three, caused by fog and darkness combined, were made in an urgent hurry. I got away with all except one, yet not without some abominably close shaves. The exception occurred in the mountains of Yugo-Slavia. Through inexperience I was caught at nightfall by the mountain mist. I landed in one big and violent hurry. There was a narrow valley there which would have done at a pinch, had it not been divided into hundreds of narrow cultivation strips. These strips are from 100 to 300 yards long, and from 10 to 30 yards wide. The idea is that each villager shall have a strip here and a strip there, in order that no man may accuse his neighbour of collaring the best land. At the last moment we came to a strip as soft as butter. I could sense Elijah's wheels sinking into it. Over she went, bang on to her nose. Again I found myself in the undignified position of dangling from my safety belt ten feet above the ground. It was too dark to assess the damage. I should have landed earlier, and would have, but judging the country by its appearance from above, I had pictured hordes of fierce mountaineers swarming out and slicing Elijah into small pieces suitable for interior decoration.

What annoyed me was the criticism of a local pilot who declared that " such a landing could not be made a second time." I offered to prove it could be—provided they would lend me a machine for the test. Ten days later I jogged on. I had adventures all the way, but have not the space to describe them. On making a forced landing near the village of Codaesti, in Moldavia, the fierce-looking peasants in their sheepskin rig-outs mistook me for a Bolshevik from over the border. A local official who spoke French arrived and explained they had been considering the advisability of shooting me; to which I replied that I had had nothing to eat all day and asked them kindly to defer any frivolous debates till after dinner. This suggestion worked wonders; they entertained me nobly to " goulatsch," and organised a hilarious party to follow, the whole population flattening their noses in turn against the only window-pane.

At another town in this part of the world I was the guest of an officer with the most hospitable nature one could conceive of. After introducing me to a delightfully entertaining Russian belle, he was always willing to work in his cold office adjoining the most comfortable Orientally-furnished salon while ' la belle Russe ' discussed with me in German questions of international importance. Unfortunately my German vocabulary is very limited.

The following is a translation of a paragraph in the " Bukaresti Dimineata " of the 14th November, 1929 :—

" Jassy, 12th November.

" An English aeroplane landed here yesterday for a short visit, piloted by Mr. Chicesterc of New Zealand, director of the Godvin Chicesterc Aviation Co. of London.

" Mr. Chicesterc is flying one of the Company's planes. He left New Zealand last week, touched at London, then at Paris, where he picked up another aviator. He continued over Milan to Jugo-Slavia. Then on approaching Zagreb his propeller broke at a height of some hundreds of feet and the aviators were in great danger. The pilot succeeded in landing near the Zagreb airport, and after repairs continued towards Roumania.

" The aeroplane, of unusual shape and colour,

IN THE MOUNTAINS OF JUGO-SLAVIA

Facing page 34

attracted crowds to the aerodrome of Tecuci. At Vaslui the pilot met with fog, and was obliged to make a forced landing near Codaesti. Leaving his machine, he presented himself before the authorities at Codaesti. After satisfactory explanations he flew on to Jassy accompanied by Advocate Popovitch, Mayor of Codaesti. At Jassy the aviator was met by the whole corps of officers, headed by Major Argeseanu, Aviation Group Commander, and a reception was given in his honour. After inspecting the hangars Mr. Chicesterc left for Warsaw and London."

After another landing which I made in a field near Osnabruck on November 17th, I stayed the night with a small farmer who had fought against the New Zealanders at Dixmude. He was most hospitable, and we all spent the night under the same roof, papa, mama, the kids, grand-papa, grand-mama, myself, Elijah, and five cows, Elijah and the coos occupying the hall.

Incidentally I obtained valuable experience about legal formalities when flying over foreign countries. At every landing the following authorities must be interviewed and satisfied as to the pilot's bona fides :—Police, Customs, military, air force, and aerodrome officials. Passports, permits to fly the plane in each country and carnet de passage de douanes must be examined. The carnet de passage enables the bearer to take a plane into a country and out again without paying Customs duty on the plane.

In sum, I soon discovered the only way to fly across a country quickly was to avoid landing in it. In addition I found it difficult to obtain petrol and oil supplies with any expedition. I nearly

35

always had to wait a long time for petrol, once 16 hours. At first I considered myself lucky to get one meal a day, until I got wise enough always to carry a loaf of bread with me. This I would gnaw at odd moments.

On re-crossing the Channel after some thousands of miles travelling over difficult terrain, I was content with a height of 50 feet above the water. I am sorry Joe could not see it.

CHAPTER III

IT was November 20th when I returned to England. For the next four and a half weeks life became strenuous.

My partner had sent the £400. Alas! half was already spent!

My diary of November 21st reads:—

"Extremely depressed this morning on getting Goodwin's telegram, 'Advise selling plane expensive salvage Malay aerodromes. No more money possible, all reserves used up, expected £2,000 loan unavailable, last money sent.' Add to the money worry the constant query as to whether I can pull off the flight when so many old experienced pilots have crashed—the constant fear of breaking the machine again—the overwhelming amount of detail yet to be arranged. Felt so down in the dumps that I rushed off to business. Inquired re rubber boat. Saw Air Ministry re route. Paid £20 towards telegraphing for plane permits to fly over Egypt, Iraq, Persia, India, Strait Settlements, Portuguese Timor, Dutch East Indies, etc. They say they can't possibly have the Egyptian permit for three weeks. Ordered maps, discussed insurance with Champneys, discussed tanks with De Havilands. They can put in two more tanks to give a total of 59 gallons. At 14 miles per gallon, this will give a range of 826 miles. Total load with boat will then be about 1,750-1,800 lbs. The plane weighs 915 lbs. Have cast the die now, although I won't have enough cash."

Every day I had as much or more to do than described in this day's work. That $4\frac{1}{2}$ weeks' work was exhausting always, boring and worrying mostly, and exciting sometimes. In addition I was weighed down with the feeling that it was all futile, the presentiment that I was going to crash and that all this forethought, organisation, hard work and expense, was so much useless waste.

The only spark of cheeriness was that the Air Ministry seemed as keen to help me as I was to be helped.

I settled down to hard work. The daily routine scarcely varied. A trip to the Air Ministry at Gwydyr House, where I would get a scrap or two of information about aerodromes or possible routes. Visits to various petrol companies, finally ending by one company undertaking to lay down supplies for me for 2/6 a gallon right through. The day's information from Gwydyr House would lead me to the map shop, where I would purchase a few more maps; thence to the petrol company to discuss the relative merits of two landing-fields from the point of view of laying down supplies. Perhaps a talk with Mr. Bentley, who has twice flown from London to the Cape and back, to discuss long cross-country work. Or Captain Jones, late Director of Civil Aviation of Australia, about Australian conditions, and flying in the Tropics. A few visits to shops for the acquisition of more equipment. A trip to De Havilands to barney about the price of a different kind of tank or spare parts. A visit to the Government Meteorological

38

Any communications on the
subject of this letter should be
addressed to :—
THE SECRETARY,
AIR MINISTRY,
GWYDYR HOUSE,
WHITEHALL,
S.W.1

and the following number quoted —

C.A. 4

AIR MINISTRY,.
GWYDYR HOUSE,
WHITEHALL,
LONDON, S W.I.

19th December, 1929

Proposed Flight to Australia.

Sir,

With reference to previous correspondence
addressed to you regarding the renewal of rebellion
activities on the North African Coast, I am directed to
inform you that a notification has now been received by
this Ministry to the effect that the situation in
CIRENAICA is such that it is unsafe for aircraft to fly
over or to make forced landings in the area extending from
BENGASI to CIRENE. It is further reported that rebel
activity extends as far as the coast and that all roads
are closed.

It would be advisable to regard the whole of
the district from BENGASI to TOBRUK as unsafe at present,
in view of the fact that the seat of operations may change
from day to day.

In the event of any British personnel landing
in the area in question they should impress upon the
natives their nationality by proclaiming that they are
"Ingliz" in view of the fact that the natives have the
greatest respect for the British and would probably treat
them well if assured of their nationality.

I am, Sir,
Your obedient Servant,

for Deputy Director of Civil Aviation.

F.C. Chichester, Esq.,
c/o Brooklands School of Flying,
Brooklands,
Byfleet, Surrey.

Facing page 38

Office to discuss general weather conditions likely to be met with.

The task was to co-ordinate the information obtained. It was a job of weeks to collect all the information about aerodromes, landing-grounds, and routes. Yet the petrol company must have several weeks' notice to lay down supplies in out-of-the-way spots. I must decide quickly questions about tanks; and the aeroplane manufacturers required twenty-one days' time for altering my plane. I spent every day rushing round like a dog with a hot tail. At night I'd work on my maps, and draw up a new schedule of halting spots, incorporating whatever fresh information I had that day obtained. I drew up a schedule showing how much I must alter my clock at different places. It would be bad business if darkness overtook one 60 miles from an aerodrome, because one had forgotten that 40 minutes of daylight would be lost through travelling Eastward.

All the while, I was scheming to ease the financial situation. I brightened up a little when the petrol company agreed to give me six months' tick for petrol and oil supplies. This gave me breathing space as far as £175 was concerned. I next tried to get credit for the fitting of my extra tanks, which with a top overhaul and some spare parts would amount to over £100. Having already spent more than £1,000 with the firm, and considering that they would benefit enormously were I successful, I started out full of hope. Here there was nothing doing. Nor was I any more successful when I suggested that a little commission would not be amiss for the sale of three planes in Roumania for which I considered myself responsible.

Times was 'ard. When a few bob could be heard jingling in my pocket, I'd send a cable to my partner, offering bright suggestions for raising a little more wind. Luckily one of these drew blood and £150 arrived. This he had raised by blistering a house of mine with a second mortgage. I breathed again. I should be able to get away now, even if I had to leave with only a little pocket money. A wreck would upset the financial as well as the actual apple-cart, but what more could one do? Then occurred the insurance nightmare. The finance company that had lent me money on the security of the plane refused to allow it to leave the country without a guarantor to guarantee repayment of the money. Worse still, it must be insured. God tempers the wind, etc. Just when I needed help most I found another supporter in Mr. Champneys of an insurance broking firm. The idea of insuring anybody for this trip was bad enough, but the suggestion of insuring a mug-pilot for it was enough to make the stately halls of Lloyds ring with cries of " Sacrilege ! " I think the successful conclusion of the 4,000 mile European flight alone saved my bacon. I was just beginning to devise fresh schemes, when Captain Lamplugh offered Mr. Champneys terms of insurance which just satisfied the finance company. Yet I had to bear the first £275 of any loss, so it did not give me much additional chance of final success should I crack up en route. As for the guarantee, in N.Z. I could have fixed it in thirty minutes, with any one of at least ten people, but in England I lacked that sort of friend. Ultimately one of my relations consented to undertake the responsibility.

My maps were going ahead well, if slowly.

SOLO TO SYDNEY

From London to Rangoon I obtained excellent millionth scale maps, that is of 15.83 miles to the inch; but from Rangoon to Darwin, the best I could get were 64 miles to the inch, and from Darwin onwards, 45 miles to the inch. I think I had 41 maps altogether. The first thing to do was to mark in the position of every landing-ground I knew of. Where possible I checked up its latitude and longitude. Then I studied the maps carefully to decide definitely which route to follow. Then came meticulous perusal of the route, to decide where lay the easiest terrain for the actual flight; whether to fly on this or that side of such and such mountain or chain of hills, where-abouts to cross this stretch of water. I marked in ink the course I thought it best to follow. The experience gained through the trip round Europe made me very fussy about this. As I knew I should never have a chance of studying the day's maps before leaving the ground, I set about learning by heart as much as possible of the route before leaving England. I joined all the maps together, and cut them into a strip nine inches wide, centring about the projected course. This strip I divided into five portions, small enough to fit on to the rollers of my map-case. The total length of the five pieces was $71\frac{1}{2}$ feet. I went over them all, first marking the magnetic variation every few hundred miles, next working out the magnetic bearing of each change in direction; again, marking in the final compass course; again, measuring all distances. During this process, I marked off every 40th mile peg (so to speak). I have found this a valuable help in indicating approximately what one's position should be every half-hour after taking off. Then I went all over everything again

41

to make as certain as possible. I used to reckon it was a ten-hour job to work through the maps for each fresh requirement.

In choice of places as petrol dumps, I was largely influenced by my desire to try and beat Hinkler's record. I say record, because although Hinkler was at that time the only man who had made this flight solo, he did it in " record " time. It will be interesting to see how long it remains unbroken. I had always had the intention to try for a record, unless or until I had an accident; when that happened I would, if still able, amble along at leisure.

He had averaged 640 miles a day. It was not much use trying to beat his time by a few hours, so I divided the distance as nearly as possible into 500 mile stages. I would try to make two of these stages each day. To do this would necessitate a daily average of 12½ hours in the air, and the only way to manage that would be to leave every morning in the dark, at about 2 o'clock. So I went along to the Air Ministry again and enlisted their aid to obtain permission from England, France and Italy to fly over these countries at night without navigation lights. To fit navigation lights on a Moth would be akin to supplying a steamer's anchor to a five ton yacht. For ten days previous to leaving, I used to get up every morning at 2 o'clock and work on maps, Elijah and what-not. This was to get my eye in, so to speak.

The following is the list of gadgets I bought or collected for installing in my cockpit, so that they should always be within my reach :—

One knife.

42

One pocket compass.
Two pairs of goggles.
One spare pair of spectacles.
Maps.
Pair dividers.
Ruler.
Douglas protractor.
Course and distance calculator.
Torch and spare battery.
Log book.
Journey log book.
Carnet-de-passage.
Passport.
Pilot's license.
Permit to fly over country.
Route information.
Coffee and water.
Bread, butter, cheese, dates, fruit, meat.
Cigarette lighter.
Helmet.
Scarf.
Sidcote suit.
Sheepskin boots.
Cotton wool.
Clock.
Atlas.

The following equipment I collected to carry in the front cockpit :—

Complete tool kit.
63 spare parts, varying from piston rings to an inner tube.
Blankets.
Rubber boat complete with mast, sail and oars.
Pump for same.

43

Rope.
Dunlop repair outfit.
Air pistol.
Screw pickets.
Engine, propeller, and cockpit-covers.
Spare oil.
Hatchet.
Razor and gear.
Hair brush, etc.
Spare shirt.
Spare underwear.
Spare stockings.
Spare trousers.
Mackintosh.
Goloshes.
Pair shoes.
A box to carry the eight plugs not in use.
Candle.
Antiseptic soap.
Sheepskin coat.
Emergency ration of tinned black bread (Pumpernickel) in case of sea voyage in the rubber boat.

SOLO TO SYDNEY

	Hours	Distance Miles	Petrol Gallons
London-Lyons	6½	516	40
Lyons-Pisa	6½	516	44
Pisa-Catania	7½	589	48
Catania-Home (sea trip)	4¼	341	28
Home-Benghazi (desert)	6½	520	44
Benghazi-Mersa Matruh (desert)	6½	504	44
Mersa Matruh-Gaza (desert except Nile)	6¼	480	48
Gaza-Bagdad (desert)	7¾	620	44
Bagdad-Bushire	7¼	574	48
Bushire-Jask	7	560	52
Jask-Karachi	7¾	614	48
Karachi-Nasirabad	6½	516	42
Nasirabad-Allahabad	5½	444	36
Allahabad-Calcutta	6¼	488	42
Calcutta-Akyab	5¼	408	36
Akyab-Rangoon	4½	362	44
Rangoon-Victoria Point	7¾	610	60
Victoria Point-Kwala Lampur	7	545	56
Kwala Lampur-Singapore	2¾	205	32
Singapore-Batavia	8	635	60
Batavia-Soeurabaja	5½	424	40
Soeurabaja-Bima	5¾	460	44
Bima-Atemboa	6½	510	60
Atemboa-Darwin (sea)	6½	512	52
Darwin-Brunette Downs (desert)	6¾	640	52
Brunette Downs-Cloncurry	4¾	370	36
Cloncurry-Charleville	8	625	56
Charleville-Sydney	9	720	
	180¼	14,308	1,306

45

SOLO TO SYDNEY

(1) Ask Commandant about leaving as soon as possible.
(2) Obtain meteorological report.
(3) Fill petrol and oil.
(4) Check next aerodrome position.
(5) Exercise.
(6) Check maps for next lap and forbidden areas.
(7) Stock up food, coffee and water.
(8) Ask Commandant to telegraph next Commandant.
(9) When in Africa, telegraph last 'Drome. Ask petrol agent to telegraph for food.
(10) Check time of day.
(11) Arrange boat.
(12) Clean plugs.
(13) Clean filters.
(14) Check tappet clearances.
(15) Grease and oil.
(16) Put on clock.
(17) Change plugs.
(18) Change oil.

It is almost impossible, and it would be fatiguing, to give in detail the hundreds of small jobs that had to be attended to. When I began I thought I had a fair idea of what would have to be done, but actually hundreds more things cropped up. For instance, passports—my passport had to be endorsed for 17 countries, with special visas to be collected from the Siamese, Portuguese, Egyptian, Iraqian, Persian, and Italian Embassies.

MINISTERE DES FINANCES

ADMINISTRATION DES DOUANES

.... le ....

Dans le réponse, priére de rappeler le

Nº ....

ANNEXE ....

وزارت مالیه

ادارۀ کمرکات

مورخه ۱۳

در جواب خواهشمند است نمره ذیل را تذکار نماید

نمره ....

ضمیمه ....

Nº 8172.

S. A. le Président du Conseil dit que suivant
une communication reçue du Ministère des Affaires Etrangères
la Légation d'Angleterre a demandé d'autoriser le survol du
territoire persan de l'aviateur anglais Mr.F.Chichester qui
partira seul le 17 Decembre de l'Angleterre vers l'Australie
Il exécutera un vol privé et civil atterrira à Bouchire
B/Abbass et Tchahbar. Il est monté à bord de l'avion G/AAK
De Havilland 85 H.P.Gipsy Moth Plane et il ne porte pas avec
lui d'arme de T.S.F. ou appareil photographique. Il arrivera
en Perse vers le 23 Decembre (le 2 Dey)

Ne voyant pas d'objection à ce voyage S.A.demande
de faire donner les instructions nécéssaires à ce sujet.

IND. Nº 13365.   Copie en double texte de la lettre qui
précède est adressée à Monsieur le Directeur Provincial des
Douanes à Bouchire pour information et gouverne.

Il est prié de remettre une copie de la présente
au pilote pour Bender Abbass et Tcharbar.

Téhéran, le 30 Azar 1308,
P. L'ADMINISTRATEUR GENERAL DES DOUANES
S.   DELCORDE.

IND. Nº 8050 Copie en double texte de ce qui précède est

adressée à Monsieur le Directeur Provincial des Douanes à

B/Abbass.

Bouchire, le 1er Dey 1308,
P. LE DIRECTEUR PROVINCIAL,

Facing page 46

CHAPTER IV

On Wednesday, December 18th, I took the plane over to Brooklands for the final touches.

First there were the drift lines to be painted on the wings. Nobody seemed to know anything about this, so it took a lot of time and hot air before they were finally fixed.

The idea is roughly as follows:—Suppose the plane is drifting 10°. In that case an object in the path of the plane will slip off at an angle of 10° to that path.

Sitting in the cockpit, paint a line on the wing corresponding to the path this object follows in making its 10° angle, so that after the plane has passed the object, this line on the wing will continue to point to the object.

Conversely, if you see an object emerge from under the end of the line and later notice the line still points to it, you must be drifting 10°. Similarly you paint in lines on both port and starboard wings for every 5° up to 30°.

At the end of the day the work was not much advanced. Next morning I got wind of an approaching catastrophe. The finance company was going to demand another guarantee before I could leave the country, so that in the event of a complete write-off, they would not have to wait for my £275 to come in by monthly instalments but would get it immediately in a lump sum. I

47

had about as much chance of finding a guarantor for this as of flying to the moon in a perambulator.

I rushed out and spurred on all hands, including the cook, to crack my work through as if the devil were chasing them with white-hot tongs.

There was the making of a stream-lined cover for the front cockpit, which had to be designed to lessen resistance to the wind, and at the same time I must be able to snap it open in a second to get out my boat. Then there was a hole to be cut in the back of the front cockpit so that I could keep any food in front and yet be able to withdraw it from where I sat. Then collecting and stowing of food and packing in my gear, which seemed prodigious in quantity and bulk. Urgent telephoning to the Meteorological Office and to Mr. Campbell, of Gwydyr House, to find out if the last permits were through. Yes; the Persian one had come through that morning, only the Italian permit for night flying without lights had not yet arrived.

I rushed about anxiously, pulling out my watch every few minutes and forgetting the time immediately I returned it to my pocket.

At last in desperation I had literally to tear the bus away from the mechanics. I took to the air as urgently as I could without map, almost in the dark and drifting 20° or 30° to port. I got quite nervous about finding Croydon, although it was only 15 miles away. I hadn't the foggiest memory of the configuration of the built-over country surrounding it. What a deuce of a joke if, on the point of setting out for Australia, I should get lost doing the 15 miles between Brooklands and Croydon! Yet I used to lose my way nearly every time I went over to Stag Lane from Brooklands, although I made the trip dozens of times.

Ha! at last, there were the red lights marking the edge of Croydon Aerodrome.

Immediately I landed an official came up and demanded to know why I was flying without navigation lights. I told him I had special permission, but I don't think he believed me at the time, because he returned later to say he had rung up headquarters and it was quite all right.

After fuelling with petrol and oil I collected my journey log book, carnet-de-passage, passport and license, and went off to clear the Customs and other authorities.

I was carrying my maps and a few things along to the hotel, when I remembered my thermos flask, so returned to the hangar. On the way over in the dark I asked three men strolling along whether they knew of a shop near by where I might buy some soap. One said: " To tell you the truth, we are strangers here ourselves." We walked towards the hangar. As soon as we came into the light he said: " Aren't you Chichester? Don't you remember me? I'm Waller of Hootton." After retrieving the flask we strolled back again, and he went on: " I shall always remember your turning up at Liverpool in a new machine without a compass and with that ridiculous map of yours." He said he had just flown down himself in his own kite. He asked if I had been for any more flights since. I said " Yes; I have been around Europe for a flight." " Great heavens! " I can hear his voice as I write, " But you've only just got your license, haven't you? And are you contemplating anything else in the near future? Perhaps you are going to try to fly home," he added jestingly. I replied I was, as a matter of fact. I have since been honest with myself and realise I did not want to discuss my trip with people solely for fear of ridicule. " You're not, really? " he said. " When are you starting? " I replied, " In about six hours." Whereat he was silent for some time. What a drawback seldom to be believed when one tells the naked truth! Whereas some people can tell awful crams only to have you hang on their every word and ask for more. However, he seemed presently to come to, and later insisted on making a trip into town for my soap, not to mention the proverbial corkscrew, which was the only article I had forgotten (it never got into my list somehow).

I ate dinner in a panic. When the porter came to say I was wanted on the 'phone I got hot and cold by turns. Then got angry and was unnecessarily rude to the wretched man. First I said I wouldn't answer it. Finally I did. I couldn't imagine who could be ringing me except the finance company. They must have got on my trail at Brooklands, where some silly ass must have given me away. Imagine my relief to find it was only the officer in charge of the Meteorological Office, advising me word had come through that I must not land at Grogak, Rembang, Bima, Reo or Larantoeka in the Dutch East Indies, because they were flooded. This did not leave many other landing grounds there—if any. However, it was impossible to wait till they dried up again, so I refused to worry. I rang Mr. Campbell, of Gwydyr House, who said he had at last received permission to fly over France without lights, but no word was through from Italy. I felt quite exhausted, but even so could not sleep well. I pictured a bailiff arriving at the last moment to prevent me taking the machine away.

50

SOLO TO SYDNEY

I was up at 1.30 and stowed away some bacon and eggs. Waller and his two friends arrived to give me a hand. By the time I had got the weather reports—and I did not like leaving in the dark without them—and by the time I had got the bus out of the hangar and started up, it was 2.30. A man and a girl joined the party. I asked the man if he would be so good as to walk ahead of me to the end of the aerodrome, to prevent my running into a hangar in the dark, the floodlight being out of action. The girl was particularly nice in the way she said " Good-bye " to me.

I sang out " Cheerio! " Off we went. The ground was devilish bumpy, being frozen hard. Later I found that the take-off had ripped open the tyre and tube, so no wonder she bumped so much. I had never before taken off Elijah with full load up. I estimated we had up 1,800 lbs., but doubtless I exaggerated. It was no use worrying about the weight, for either she took off or she didn't. I kept my eye on a distant street lamp. Elijah rose into the heavens. The fire was grand, like four very large blow lamps, the cylinder ports belched out their steady bluish flame. It was good company.

We woggled about a good bit at first, for this was the first time I had tried to steer a course at night. This fact might have worried me, but I reflected that other people had done it, so it must be all right. It was great. Down below I began to pick out the fields. Broad edges of hoar frost stretched along the lee of the hedges. I could see it was no good to have the machine rising and dipping and joggling about—that meant loss of time. I concentrated on keeping her head steady with this new sort of indeterminate horizon, and at the same time set about reading the drift. This was another thing I had not had time to practise before. I could plainly see the drift lines on the wings, but by the time it reached the trailing edge of the wing I could never remember what object had passed under the leading edge. Finally I decided we were drifting 25° to port, so allowed accordingly. I am now sure this was an error of about 10° too much.

We presently passed over a winking red light. I took this to be a direction beacon pointing to Lympne, and consequently imagined the course to be accurate so far. It may have been, for not long afterwards the wind dropped right away, and later still changed direction. As I did not read my drift again, having plenty else to do, I naturally did not notice the wind had changed, so that the 25° allowed for drift at the start was bound to take me 25° out of my course later. Presently the twinkling lights of a largish town came up on my port quarter. I took it to be Maidstone. If it was, I was pretty close to my desired track. The coast arrived. A large town showed—again on the port side. I took it to be Folkestone, but was surprised to be unable to find any signs of Lympne aerodrome. I was having as good sport as ever I have had.

Leaving the coast and pushing off into the murky darkness was another exciting moment. Up till now the moon had been shedding companionable light on the subject. When I was just beginning to think this night-flying to be easy money, it hid itself behind a layer of light cloud. Anything resembling horizon completely vanished, and once again Elijah began sawing the air as her nose bobbed up and down with my unskilful piloting. All I could see was a glint on a small patch of water almost directly beneath the plane. When I looked at my altimeter its dial was gaily turning round and round in giddy circles. I had fondly imagined this fault had been fixed at the aerodrome. This was decidedly unpleasant. If the waves were very small I might be only a few feet above them; if large I might be thousands of feet. I turned the dial back to zero, noted where the needle came to and then climbed 500 feet. Thereby I knew I was at least 500 feet above the sea.

F.L. No. 43: "Don't try night flying without a reliable altimeter." I might add F.L. No. 44: "Don't fly by night without a lighted instrument board." The luminous compass was plainly visible, but my 1/3 torch only worked in spasms and frequently needed to be opened for the insertion of a piece of rag in the bottom, otherwise it wouldn't work. Not that I used it much at this time, I was too busy alternately watching the patch of water below and searching the darkness ahead for any signs of a cliff. After twelve minutes I redoubled my efforts to see land ahead. After fifteen minutes without any signs I became anxious. Had the wind increased in strength? Was I being blown along parallel to the Belgian coast? Black and impenetrable as it was ahead, I feared to quit for any length of time my look-out for land. Had I possessed a one-piece map showing the whole of South England with the French and Belgian coasts, I would have seen quickly the improbability of drifting into the North Sea. Had there been time to use the ruler and protractor I should have seen it with the map I had, but, as I say, I thought it too risky to leave the look-out while I manipulated the torch, the map, the ruler and protractor, be-

sides the controls. I could have climbed another
3,000 or 4,000 feet and flown blind, but that meant
losing sight of the glimmering patch of sea below.
Also I wished to know when we approached land.
Then too, flying blind for several hours might
bring me out at daylight over a fog-bank or low
cloud-bank, resting on some chain of hills. Half
an hour went by and still not a sign of anything
above or below save the patch of sea. At least I
had by now made up my mind that it was impossible that I was travelling up to the North Sea; we
must needs be headed southwards into the Dieppe
Bay. I believed that by changing course to eastwards we must shortly strike the coast. But I
decided to carry on for three reasons. Firstly,.in
spite of my decision that I was on a good course,
there might yet be some mistake, in which case
it was better not to zig-zag about in the dark.
Secondly, by continuing southwards we were head-
ing towards Lyons, and travelling eastwards meant
so much loss of time. Thirdly, I felt the coast of
France was offering me a personal slight by not
appearing and it seemed wrong to give way to its
whims by changing course.

After three-quarters of an hour above the water
we flew over the lights of several vessels. It was
difficult to tell in the dark what they were, but I
guessed them to be small fishing trawlers. If they
were, I was probably about 800 feet above the
water. The altimeter read 5,500. In flying, when
you ought to be in sight of some object and can't
see it, every minute seems an age. I don't think
it is the right philosophy which prompts me to look
ahead for landmarks when flying. I believe one
ought always to carry on until something turns up
and then see what it is. But it is rather disturbing

54

for a novice who is crossing a comparative ditch like the Channel and expecting to be over it in 15 minutes, to find himself still wandering over the sea after 55 minutes, especially if he knows how utterly helpless he will be if the compass has gone wrong and he is headed into the Atlantic without one.

An hour after leaving England land suddenly loomed up just ahead, in the shape of a high whitish cliff—I was just about on the level with the top of it. I flew along beside its dim ghostly white face and read the compass bearing of its direction. Continuing for another five miles I repeated the process, getting the same bearing. I went along for another five miles : the bearing did not change. Then, studying the map by torchlight, I concluded there was only one piece of coast which this could be, namely, a stretch to the N.E. of Dieppe. I thereupon worked out the bearing of Paris from that spot and set a course accordingly. I allowed 10° for drift, but when just before dawn I got to Paris, it wasn't there, so to speak. The wind had meanwhile dropped altogether.

An almost overpowering desire to sleep attacked me at this point. This must be zero hour. A bleak dismal November grey crept into the sky, and my feelings reflected it. I was cold, cramped, and inclined to doze off. Why in the name of goodness did one make damn-fool flying expeditions when one might be lying in a comfortable feathery bed? At this moment I struck a town beside a railroad and a canal, and from them got a possible fix of my position on the map. Assuming this to be correct, I worked out the bearing of Lyons and headed straight for it. I might find it difficult to locate Lyons in the middle of France, but there is always the golden maxim to fall back on as a last resource, " When in doubt, land and ask a policeman."

Dawn broke, and very glad I was too. The earth was white with frost and all the canals and patches of water covered with ice. Not a breath of wind was stirring; the smoke lazily drifted about the chimney-tops.

Presently I was flying over some woods. They awakened memories in my brain. " Hanged if I don't know these woods," I said to myself. " If I'm right I shall find a river about a mile ahead." And sure enough there it was. It was the exact spot I had flown over in the storm when I went on that tour round Europe. There are two rivers to show the way to Lyons : this was the westerly one, the Loire.

I had a meal with coffee, which was disgustingly cold, did some physical jerks, pumped full the old cistern at the top of the house, and did a song and dance act. The dance was limited in scope to the marionette type. I wondered if the folk below could hear my little song, so I climbed up a bit in case I should be hurting their sensibilities.

We continued up the Loire to Roanne, then hopped the hills across to Lyons. To my surprise and relief I made quite a fair landing, although the machine tried to slue round on the ground. This was explained later by a mechanic when he spotted a flat tyre with a nasty gash in it. The flying since dawn had been painfully simple, but I was devilish glad to get a chance to stretch my legs. The first thing I did was to double as fast as I could in my big sheepskin boots to a point about 300 yards distant. I felt quite pleased with life, for I had been in the air seven hours without great discomfort, and thereby removed the doubt as to whether I could stand up to the nerve strain of long periods in the air. It is the vibration and noise which cause the nervous fatigue, and I cannot help wondering if one would not escape this if the propeller and engine were behind one instead of in front.

I ate an enormous omelette and washed it down with red wine, while I enquired about the route over the Alps. A pilot who had crossed them told me something about the route, stressing the fact that I must cross at not less than 10,000 feet. This was rather peeving, for I was not sure Elijah could do it with full load up. After the omelette they procured me a weather report, which said the Alps crossing was all clear. This was grand news, for going round by Marseilles entailed an extra 180 miles.

It was very pleasant meeting again the aerodrome officials I had got quite friendly with in my previous visit here. It was after refuelling, when I was just about to climb aboard, that the flat tyre was discovered. This took an hour to repair. I'm afraid I did little except stump up and down muttering imprecations and looking at my watch every few minutes, while I calculated whether I could make Pisa before dark. At last at 12.50 I got away. Very glad I was to leave Lyons, for here it is that so many setting out on long flights to India, Australia, or South Africa come to grief. It is painful to think of how many fields round Lyons have had debris strewed in them at some time or another. My satisfaction at escaping whole from this valley of wrecks was short-lived, for the presentiment that I too would have a crash had intrenched itself so firmly during the last five

57

weeks that it quickly recovered its sway over me.

I started climbing immediately after leaving Lyons, apprehensive about the machine's climbing powers with full load and also about the effect of the bumps which I fully expected. I kept plugging away at 65—70; 6,000 feet; then 7,000 feet; the railway began to resemble a black thread. We seemed to take an age climbing each thousand feet, but that was only because I was watching the altimeter dial so closely—a watched meter never turns. The Alps presented an impenetrable snow-capped wall, backed up by innumerable humps and mounds covered in snow and stretching for a seemingly endless distance. The sun shone in flawless weather.

S.E. of Chambéry I hopped across the back of a saddle which runs down from the Aiguilles d'Avres. This was about 6,000 feet in height, and I anticipated some fearful bumps as we crossed it. Not one. I drew in great lungfuls of the crisp air when we were over. It was a great relief. The 15,782 feet of Mt. Blanc seemed at the very wing tip towering above us, yet it was actually forty miles away. Now we were abreast of the Roche Chevière. One had the feeling one must keep a good look-out for fear of running into it, yet it was half a mile away. It seemed to be higher than we were; that couldn't be the case, for we were now 9,000 feet above Lyons. Tracks were visible, no thicker than spiders' webs, zig-zagging up the mountain sides. The valley below could no longer be seen without tacking from side to side, for it lay a narrow-gutted streak right below the plane. It would have been easy to see by tilting the plane over on one side, but this I did not care to do for fear of losing any of the valuable height we had gained. We might need every inch of it if we ran into bumpy air later.

Presently, seeing a township with the absurd pin-point size of its houses making it seem almost of another world, I thought we had arrived at Modane, but later noticed the railway still beneath us. As it was unlikely to have been continued up the valley beyond Modane, I could only conclude I had made a mistake. A few minutes later I saw the line burrow into the side of a hill and knew that here was Modane for sure. We had lost forty miles in the climb. We were now 10,000 feet above Lyons. I continued to be nervous about bumpy air, for I feared we should lose 200 or 300 feet of height at every bump with such a load; but the air was remarkably still.

Suddenly I spotted a snow-cloud lying between some mountains on my right, and it put the wind mightily up me, for I supposed it to be lying on the Cenis Col. It looked to be floating just where the pass should be. Should I be able to take some other crossing? Maybe, but the idea of wandering among unknown Alps in a plane did not appeal to me. How slowly the time ran as we continued up the valley, merely because of the uncertainty as to what lay ahead. Was it easy to recognise the Col? Would it be in a snow-cloud? Would there be a storm the other side? Would the clouds be sitting on the mountains the other side? We came abreast of a col on the right. Ha! Cenis! But I felt dubious and ended up by deciding to explore further before entering this one. It was just as well, for, five minutes later, a low col opened up a view of a valley below the snow-line. Cenis Col! Obviously, and easy money into the bargain! It was a long way below me: I had 3,000 feet to spare. I stuck Elijah's nose into it and scudded by an old snow-covered fort on my right at 90 m.p.h. It was a tremendous relief to find all my fears unjustified, and I paddled down that valley feeling full of song.

Susa, Turin. At Turin I noticed the wind was at last favouring me slightly. Fine! I would be in Pisa at such and such a time. Again, easy money—and so it was until we slipped through the hills to Genoa. Once feel " home " with flying and you catch it where the chicken caught the axe—in the neck. Whizz! Whop! Bump! What a trouncing we got! Each bump sent a shower of petrol into my face from the vent of the front cockpit tank. I slipped out over the sea only to find it worse still. Poor old Elijah! I was scared stiff she would shed a wing or two. Looping the loop was like rocking the baby compared to it for structural strain. We bolted back to the mainland again and, hurled this way and that, tossed about like a postage stamp in a gale, only just managed to clear the necessary col. I had to climb at the steepest angle possible with throttle wide open. Several times the slots clanked as an extra strong bump stalled the machine.

For a while I went down a valley parallel to the coast. At first I tried to climb in the hope that higher up we should escape the bumps; but it was impossible to rise. Each time we gained a few hundred feet a violent down wash of air would force us back to where we were before.

Then I tried the sea again; the bumps seemed to be getting a little less violent when I had to leave it to avoid the forbidden area of Spezia. I had just the same trouble to get over the hills, and when over, heavens! At one moment I feared

60

we were going to be sat right on to a hill, as a current of air bore us down and down and down. I kept as hot as if I had just run a mile race. I'm afraid I cussed the Italian Government into ten other worlds for making me dodge Spezia.

Night fell. The wind calmed itself again. But I had " missed the bus " through it. I plodded on to Pisa, which could be recognised by its lights miles ahead. I had carefully memorised the position of the aerodrome before daylight ended. I saw it, splendidly lit, a long way ahead, complete with a beautiful searchlight signalling me. I came up to it, cut my motor three times to let them know I had arrived, and then shut off to land. Close to the ground I found the lights were bright lamps illuminating a long L-shaped hoarding which bordered perhaps half a mile of the side of one street and a quarter of a mile of the side of another at right angles. A perfect landing " L." The searchlight was a powerful motor-car.

I began the aerodrome hunt, but did not have far to go, for I soon picked it up—a big black space with the white landing " T " faintly visible on it by contrast, but not a light in the whole show except from a barracks at one end. I set about making the best of a bad job. My first shot was a dud. I bumped and went off again, visioning a lost under-carriage and all sorts of other horrors. My next shot I faked a pretty fair landing, but it was ticklish work in the dark. I seemed fated not to meet a lighted aerodrome.

After landing I started to taxi in; the field was boggy and I got stuck in the mud. A swarm of soldiers seemed to spring out of the ground and burst a rib or two of my leading-edge in helping me out of the mud. I asked about the lights.

"Ah! les illuminations, mais oui, certainement nous en avons de très belles, mais nous n'avons pas cru que vous pourriez arriver si tôt et encore nous pensions que vous feriez le tour de l'aérodrome pendant une demi-heure que nous chercherions le garde-lumière."

And then the fun began. My French is the world's worst after a few hours in the air. My wants were simple enough, merely petrol, oil, work on the motor, sleep, food, and a 2 a.m. start. It took me 4½ hours' solid talk and argument to arrange everything bar the sleep.

The commandant was away; I couldn't possibly leave before nine next morning, and so on. They were extraordinarily kind and helpful, but everything seems to be open to discussion at some length in Italy. In the end they just could not do enough for me; only it was tiring work. We chased round the town; they found the commandant, the Customs officials, the police; they helped me change my oil, do my chores on the engine, fill up petrol, and finally lent me a camp bed. I got into it about ten o'clock, but could not sleep all at once. The trouble was I had been deuced tired before leaving England and on top of that had just put in a pretty solid twenty hours, during twelve of which I had been in the air and cut out 866 miles.

CHAPTER V

AFTER $2\frac{1}{2}$ hours' sleep I got into the air again at
1.45. It is curious to think I left without having
seen the aerodrome I landed at and took off from.
The night was lovely; everything went well till we
neared Naples. Here frequent flashes of sheet
lightning ahead disturbed my peace of mind. Then
the sky became overcast. It was like flitting along
under the ceiling of a wide, low-roofed cavern. I
saw a biggish cloud very close to the ground.
Presently I noticed it was sitting on a hill. It
looked ominous and somnolently powerful. Then
I had an idea and verified it with a map. It was
no other than friend Vesuvius. What a magnificent sight when I got closer! The dark billowy
smoke rolling heavily away as if slowly expelled
from the lungs of a colossal Cyclops lying on his
back. The million sparkling and twinkling lights
clustering round the bay at the foot of the volcano.
On the shoulder of a hill I saw two lights moving,
one up and the other down in a peculiar manner
with snapping flashes of strong white light. This
puzzled me at first until I thought of a funicular;
that seemed to explain away the phenomenon to my
satisfaction.

I hopped across a peninsula between Naples and
Salerno, but it was very unpleasant. A black
cloud the other side made it very difficult to distinguish between the 4,000 foot hill and the sky;
after the saddle I seemed to be flying in pitch

63

darkness. I came to a big storm cloud bursting with electricity. The flashes of sheet lightning momentarily lit up the whole sea; fortunately I was able to dodge it. A little later I was not so lucky with a rain cloud. I was right into it before I knew of its proximity. The rain was not heavy, but I couldn't see six feet in front of me. I shut off the engine and glided down at a steep angle, nervous lest we hit the deck before catching sight of it. It was a great relief when we got through the cloud and the hills became visible again. Visible is not truly correct, for they were distinguishable solely by their utter blackness in comparison with the not so black sea and atmosphere. Earlier in the night we had been flying along a coast sparkling with lights like a Christmas tree, but now we were evidently abreast of barren and mountainous country.

I began to feel sleepy, and when the dirty grey storm clouds behind the mountains, beginning to cut out their skyline, warned me of approaching daybreak, the sleepiness became an agony. I moved about in every conceivable way, waved my arms, jumped up and down in the seat, stamped my feet. If I jumped up I was asleep before I landed back in the seat. If I jerked my head forward I was asleep before I could reverse the movement. Something inside me felt stark, primeval, elemental. As I lookd out at the black masses of towering mountains, at the rugged grey rock precipices, many hundred feet high, dropping sheer into the sea, and, on the other side, the dull glazed surface of the Mediterranean stretching out of sight under a ceiling of threatening clouds, I felt myself as a spectator at the very beginning of creation.

The process of falling asleep was queer. The

motor explosions would completely separate them-selves in my hearing. Usually I heard four ex-plosions entirely isolated, which is extraordinary when you think of the infinitesimal lapse of time between the explosions, completely indistinguish-able by the ordinary everyday part of the brain.

Each time the interval increased in length. Bang . . . . Bang . . . . . . Bang . . . . Bang . . . . then complete silence. I would wake with a jolt, petrified with fear that the engine had stopped. The first half-dozen times I could not believe that it had not. Then I realised it was a hallucination, but this only made things worse. Before that, the shock which each awaken-ing dealt me had scared my nerves into watchful-ness for a certain period. Now that fear was removed. Day broke; I had been about six hours flying and had covered about four hundred miles in the dark.

I took off my helmet and goggles and draped my head in the slipstream.

I tried watching the ground, but couldn't distin-guish anything clearly because my eyes would not align when I was able to keep them open.

I wrote a note, tried to study the map, had some food, drank a lot of cold water, and did everything I could think of to keep myself occupied.

I was sorely tempted to search out one of the three landing grounds located on the foreshore when it widens sufficiently. The idea of landing, of the machine coming to a standstill, of being able to loll my head against the cockpit edge and sleep on, made me ache all over. But we were past the first of these landing grounds, and when we came to the second it was half washed away. Then, at the arch of the toe of Italy, the sleepiness abated and I carried on for years and years till, over the Straits of Messina, Mount Etna's 10,700 feet came up close. With her enormous, solid and rather dull snow-cap, she reminded me of a big, fat char-woman dressed up for church in a large floppy white Jugoslavian head-dress, or was it an over-boiled suet pudding which had collapsed?

It was interesting to watch the clouds forming on its snow-covered heights. Clear and cloudless air was coming in from the Mediterranean. Coming into contact with the snow a midget of a cloud formed no bigger than a pin-point. This went rolling and bowling across the snowfield, gathering size every second like a snowball, till finally a big cumulus cloud broke away from the other end of the snowfield.

At Catania, in Sicily, I made a bad landing down wind. It began all right, but got rabbity at the finish. I was much annoyed. Then began again what I call the Italian struggle. No petrol in the field, no Customs, no nothing. However, the pilots were jolly good to me, and they gave me an excellent meal. One officer lent me his room for ten minutes' sleep. I exceeded the time and had actually fifteen minutes (I might have slept for an hour).

After I had got everything ready I found my journey log-book had been taken into the town, and I had to wait nearly an hour for its re-appearance. I asked carefully about night-landing facilities at Homs, on the North African coast, some seventy miles east of Tripoli, and was assured they were all that could be desired for that purpose. There was an aerodrome there thoroughly equipped with a " phare " and all night-landing facilities.

It was obvious that I could not get there before

dark. I had landed at 9.45, and I got away at
one o'clock. My drift was 10° up to an occasional
15°. After leaving Sicily for the 285 mile water-
jump I allowed 10° and decided to keep to the right
if I came to any obstruction, as this would be
equivalent to a degree or so more. I dodged one
big storm cloud in this way, but I had to fly so
much to westwards to dodge it that when I reached
Malta I struck the island at the west end. The
idea of stopping at Malta occurred to me, but I
could not resist going on. I wanted to reach
Africa in two days.

Storms were increasing in frequency again.
They were composed of long lines of blackish cloud
raining from their middles. They looked easy to
circumnavigate, but when it came to doing it you
would swear they were racing you. I usually
altered course some 15 to 20°, expecting to get
round the storm after going a mile or two. It
was decidedly irritating to find it still ahead after
from 10 to 15 miles. One I struck was a brute.
I could see a break in it apparently quite near.
But every time I came abreast of where the opening had been, it had moved on. I think its storm
content was unrolling itself in front of me and
against the wind at the rate of 60 or 70 m.p.h. It
looked as if I would end up in Cairo if I went on
much longer, so I picked a piece close at hand
where it was almost clear and made a bolt to go
through. It turned out to be juicy hail. I did not
like that because I did not know how it would
affect my naked wooden prop, so I cut the revs.
down in case. Then there was a hefty flash of
lightning apparently close on my port wing. Old
Elijah rocked. I didn't like that either, for how
did I know what effect lightning would have on

my magnetos and compass? There occurred to me the case of the Imperial Airways plane flying down the Persian Gulf. It was flying through a storm, when suddenly it was caught in an electrical discharge. Immediately the whole plane was magnetised. The magnetos were not affected, but the compass was as useless for its purpose as a bar of soap. The pilot was fortunate in being over land at the time and not over water. The curious part about the incident was that try as they would they were unable to demagnetise the plane afterwards. They even passed the whole affair through huge hoop magnets without result. Finally they were compelled to dismantle it, remove every piece of susceptible metal and demagnetise each separately.

Fortunately after this storm the weather for the last 120 miles was pretty fine. The sun set magnificently. I was getting more accustomed to my drift lines. They always say you cannot tell drift over sea. So, although I checked time after time and reckoned the drift was 20° to port—though sometimes a few degrees less and once for a minute or two actually a few degrees to starboard—for fear I was mistaken I decided, like an M.P., to take no action in the matter.

But I made a calculation of where I should come out if I was right. I was aiming six degrees W. of Homs and a further ten degrees W. for drift. So if my drift were 20 degrees to the E., I should come out a few miles to the E. of Homs —four degrees to the east—as my friend Mr. Euclid would say. Anyway the first things I saw were a few lights and a phare twinkling just where they should be according to my calculations, so I altered course to make for them.

SOLO TO SYDNEY

I got quite a kick out of my first sight of Africa, but was very peeved to see lights twinkling in such a fashion as showed the terrain sloping steeply from the sea at that point, whereas I had expected to find a broad sea front of perfectly level sand. When I reached the town I concluded I had made a mistake, because it was so ridiculously small, and there was no sign of an aerodrome. I went on for some six to eight miles till I had turned the next corner of the coast.

I continually looked back, and observed a fairly bright reddish light, which was easily stronger than anything else I could see. Maybe the aerodrome had been on holiday and now had returned to switch on the light. When I turned the corner there was not a light in sight for Heaven only knows how many miles. I turned back to investigate the red light. It seemed ages before I reached it, and when I did I was disgusted to find it appeared to be a bonfire made by some Arab peasants (or whatever they are). Later it transpired it was a bonfire lit to light up the aerodrome for me.

Anyway I did not fancy crashing about in the underbrush where some blighter was burning his cast-off clothing, so I turned again and paddled off westward. I worked it out if I did not get rattled I should surely find a perch before Tripoli, and if not, why worry? I knew Tripoli was a war-base aerodrome for the Italians, and I guessed it would be replete with every modern convenience. Anyway I had almost, if not quite, enough juice to reach Tunis.

Darkness. Not a light on the coast. I missed the numerous lights of the Italian coast. Then I got into a cloud and could see nothing. I did not like that, as several times I thought I was just running into a hill. Here is my advice to the young: Don't have a dud altimeter for night-flying.

So I piled on another 2,000 feet in case of accidents. I always imagined the African coast to be as flat as a pancake. Presently I spotted a searchlight ahead, and it flashed and flashed, and flashed. So I reckoned it was an aerodrome signalling me, and it warmed up the cockles of my heart. A quarter of an hour later I could see a magnificent cordon of lights. The aerodrome was done up like a circus. I sang my favourite ditty. Some time later the lights appeared just as far off.

When I finally arrived I was disgusted to find the aerodrome to be a harbour, and the searchlight a phare on the Mole. I felt annoyed. I began to circle over the town. This must be Tripoli. If someone could not produce an aerodrome for me I would land in their best street. Presently a starry light flashed at me from where the aerodrome should be ten miles to the west of the town. I scuttled over to it. I cut my motor and investigated. There were no boundary lights. I glided down close to the ground. It was only a confounded motor car switching its lights off and on while it tried to pass another. I wished I had had a bomb.

Then a real pukka searchlight appeared in the sky to the east of the town. No possible mistake could there be this time, so I pelted back again. There were no boundary lights—only the solitary searchlight. It was well manipulated. Only if I landed along its beam I had to land right into the hangars, which I did not like. I gauged the dis-

70

tance between the searchlight and the hangars, judging it by the soldiers' quarters behind the hangars. I judged there was only 200 yards between the light and the hangars. Not enough room for me to get off again should I not make a perfect landing. And it was very unlikely that I would make a good landing first shot after so long in the air and in the dark on a strange 'drome.

I circled the field once or twice; I could just distinguish a splendid square of ground enclosed by trees and the hangars. I noticed plenty of water lying about, but did not worry much about it, having in mind that water makes sand hard. I decided to land 100 yards short of the searchlight. I cut my revolutions down to 1,500, and went round again at 60 to get my eye in. Then I approached to land. The next instant there was a wonk, which is the noise an aeroplane makes when it goes over on to its nose. I was jolted forward and found myself in the undignified position of dangling ten feet above the ground. I felt jolly annoyed at making a fool of myself.

I could feel the safety belt tight about my middle. Dead silence had succeeded to the roar of the engine. I was aware of the silence in spite of the rhythmic engine beat which seemed to continue not only in my brain, but in every part of my body. Nerves affected I suppose. I fumbled with the safety belt catch and pulled it. I was standing on the rudder bar and keeping my shoulders off the instrument-board with one hand. I scrambled out, put a foot on one of the centre section struts, thence jumped to the ground. To my amazement I landed with a splash. " Bless my soul," I thought, " I'm in the sea; how on earth did I get here? " I tried to remember the few

71

minutes prior to landing, to recall if there had been
any possibility of my landing in the sea. I listened,
but could hear no waves. I couldn't be bothered
to think further about it. The water was just to
my ankles. I started towards the searchlight; a
few steps, and I floundered in to my knees, but,
falling forward, touched a bank. I climbed up it;
it was only a foot or so high. I felt like Puss-in-
boots in the sheepskin thigh-boots, and had taken
enough exercise for a while, so I fumbled among
my pockets and filled my pipe, but couldn't get it
alight with the cigarette lighter.

The searchlight beam left its resting-place and
flickered round. Presently it caught the plane and
fixed on it. Elijah looked very sick. Waves in
the fabric on the top wing, the same on the bottom
wing, a rent with a strut sticking through it. Complete write-off, I thought, and looked the other
way. I wanted a light for my pipe.

Presently I looked round again and was astonished to see the silhouette of a war-dance thrown
on to Elijah by the beam. Dozens of people
dancing hard. It showed their legs lifting like
marionettes. It was weird. There was no sound,
just this silent private screen-projection on Elijah's
back. Presently I heard the thumping of countless
feet, yet no other sound, not a shout, not a word.
At last the phenomenon was explained when 30 or
40 soldiers came running to the ditch separating
them from the bank where I stood. They rushed
off to the side, found a crossing, then rushed up to
me. Then they all began chattering like fun and
pawed me, as if unable to believe their eyes that
I was alive. One chap could speak French, so I
asked him to leave someone to guard the plane.
Then I borrowed a match, and we set off for the

searchlight. Presently we came to an officer—the commandant—Colonel Ranza. Taking me into a bare room, he explained this was the mess, but said that all the officers returned to Tripoli for dinner in the evening. He himself had motored out as soon as he heard my machine. He had brought with him his wife, who was extraordinarily attractive and pleasant. I was a queer object for society, unshaven, dirty, wet to the knees. My eyes kept on closing with sleep as I talked. We had two or three drinks and some German sausage arrived. I thought how awful it would have been had I been on the water-wagon. By now I was just about asleep where I stood. I told the Colonel my bus was a complete write-off, and asked permission to sleep on the aerodrome that night. An orderly took me along to the room of a pilot absent in the interior, where there were pictures of Arab girls in the scantiest garb possible. I must have fallen asleep looking at them, for when, some four hours later, I woke up to find myself groping along the wall, I still had my spectacles on. I was in the middle of a fierce nightmare. I dreamt I was flying when suddenly all visibility totally disappeared, so that I could no nothing but wait for a crash.

The next morning the orderly came to wake me up. I wished him to perdition. Never had I enjoyed a sleep so much. His entry was accompanied by such a wealth of gesticulation that I fancied something must be in the wind. The Italians are very different from their neighbours, the Slovenians, when it comes to languages. Whereas the Slovak frequently knows three or even four languages, very few Italians know any other tongue but their own. A few speak pretty bad French. In fact, they are no better linguists than the British.

When I reached the aerodrome, there was Elijah a few yards away being wheeled in by a number of soldiers. An N.C.O. named Marzocchi, who spoke French, told me she was quite undamaged except for a broken prop and front interplane strut. Frankly I didn't believe him. I had been wondering whether salvage of the fuselage would repay the cost of freighting it to England. When I inspected for myself I found he was right. My amazement was only equalled by my joy. The interplane strut had smashed through the fabric of the upper wing, but it had only grazed the main wing spar. I have never been able to make up my mind to this day whether I was lucky or unlucky about that accident. They found wheel marks in the lake bottom for 35 yards behind the plane. Flying in at landing angle I had touched without knowing it. The lake floor is as smooth as a table and the water acted as a cushion. In fact the landing must have been nearly finished before she nosed over. Had I not been keeping the tail up thinking we were still in the air it is doubtful if she would have nosed over at all. On the other hand had we touched fifty yards later we would have struck the ditch and bank, and certainly have somersaulted. I can quite understand my mistaking in the dark the salt pan for part of the aerodrome, and I had been quite right in assuming there was not much room between the searchlight and the hangars.

I may say that after all I got none of the satisfaction I had anticipated out of reaching Africa in two days—a distance of 1,906 miles, the second day's run having amounted to 1,040.

ELIJAH IN THE SALT PAN

Facing page 74

CHAPTER VI

Everybody was exceedingly good to me at Tripoli.
The British Pro-Consul, Johnny Ghirlando, came
out in the afternoon and motored me the ten miles
into town. Johnny is Maltese by birth; he had
numbers of brothers, uncles, aunts, not to mention
cousins. Nearly every day the whole family used
to foregather at the house of one of them. He
helped me cable for spare parts and generally
showed me round the town. Then there were
amusing moments to be had with the Italian pilots.
Most of them sleep in town and travel out to the
'drome by bus at 7.30 or later in the morning.
There was Vallerani, in charge of the engineering
section. He presumed I would write a book when
I had finished my flight. To write a book afterwards was the only reason Englishmen made
flights. When he found out this was the third
time I had nosed-over in Elijah he suggested I
should call it " How to Capot," by One Who
Knows. He also invented a wire cage to fasten in
front of the propeller, to protect it next time we
capoted. Alternatively he suggested a rubber propeller which would bounce without breaking when
it hit the ground. Then there was Lieut. Guidi,
whose clothes were always a marvel to behold, and
only exceeded in handsomeness by his looks. He

had an amazing collection of girls' photographs in his room—all signed. I am sure any one of these girls would have got placed in an international beauty competition. One of his interesting possessions was his hair net. I always had a desire to try it on, but never had the courage to ask. I used to call him " Topsy." My own name was " Meester Wheesky." Not because I drank it, for I think they all liked it much better than I did, but I think every Britisher is " Meester Wheesky " to them. They trotted me round to see some of their girls. There was an extraordinarily good-looking Arab girl I remember; she had short curly negro's hair, but her features and figure were superb. All the same I think her looks were the best part about her. Her religion provided a serious barrier to her being more interesting. The good class girls one never seems to meet à deux : they are chaperoned with mid-Victorian care.

Vallerani showed me a lot of interesting photos of bombing attacks on Arabs. One I shall never forget showed three Arab traitors being strung up on gibbets. The war on the Arabs seems at first sight to be one-sided, nevertheless God help any pilot who falls into their hands. One of their favourite pastimes is to cut off some valuable parts of a prisoner's body, and after inserting them in his mouth, sew up his lips.

One day I decided to try out my collapsible rubber boat in the sea. Vallerani and a few other pilots were there. Everybody was keen to try out the boat. An orderly shouldered it, and we set off for the sea, about a mile away. Every few yards we were joined by more people, until finally on reaching the shore half the mess seemed to have collected. At close range, with quite a sea running,

76

the water did not seem nearly so attractive. Everybody showed what I considered excessive politeness, and unanimously made way for me.

After blowing up the boat I shipped the mast and pushed off. Simultaneously with the first wave filling the boat, I slid off the seat into the bottom. My plus-fours waved like seaweed under the water. Beyond doubt the makers had not exaggerated when they claimed the boat was also a bath. However, it would not sink, and after smart work with the sculls I manœuvred through the breakers and hoisted sail. It sailed splendidly down wind, but I could not make it travel into or across wind. Maybe with more practice, such as one would get if dumped into the middle of the Pacific, one would become proficient enough to steer with an oar; but I think I must get a rudder for my next model. After sailing a quarter-mile down wind it was necessary to row it back. Even against wind I believe one could make 20 miles a day in it by rowing. By the time I reached the breakers I was too cocksure, I let it get broadside on to a big one, and the whole affair turned turtle, emptying me into the ocean. The audience applauded uproariously. They expected me to die of cold, but after England the water seemed quite warm.

For several days they had been hunting for the aeroplane in which Lasalle had set out to fly from France to Indo-China. It had been seen last at Tripoli. The Italians searched for it with their own machines. In the process one, a Romeo, was smashed to smithereens. It touched the ground with one wing when going all out, and somersaulted several times. It was difficult to tell from the photographs which part of the plane was which. The escape of the pilot and mechanic was miraculous. They attributed it to the fact of the fuselage being metal instead of wood.

Finally the wreckage of Lasalle's machine was discovered along the coast near Syrte. The bodies were brought to Tripoli, and the Italians set about giving the Frenchmen a great send-off. The French Consul, M. Terver, requested me to attend as a representative of British aviators. At ten o'clock a procession formed on the mole. Every department of the Italian Administration was represented. The pilots turned up in force. The one who had crashed in the Romeo was in the same row as myself. Judging by his face he did not relish the proceedings at all. All the Consuls attended. I, in my one and only plus-four suiting, was just behind Ghirlando in top hat and full regalia. There was a large squad of soldiers, a big band, a troop of Fascists in their black shirts and betasselled caps. The coffins were mounted on gun carriages, and the procession slowly traversed the town to the Cathedral, while three Jupiter-Romeos flew up and down the street in slow formation. In the Cathedral were grouped a field gun, machine guns, crossed propellers, all covered with wreaths. The Bishop of Tripoli conducted a very impressive and ceremonious service. When one of the four censers caught alight, and after burning fiercely for a while exploded with a loud detonation, it only added to the impressiveness.

The aerodrome mess gave a luncheon in honour of the French Consul. We had a very amusing time. My propeller cage, invented by Vallerani, was the stock joke of the party. I asked the Commandant to send round a paper for all the officers to autograph. One of the orderlies was a young

Arab rebel who had been captured in a recent raid. Although only about 14 or 15, he looked as proud and fierce as he looked fine. It was impossible not to feel sorry for him, carrying round wine and dishes. All the same he would be an awkward problem potting at you with a rifle behind a hydrangea bush. I got him to affix his signature among the others. After lunch, everybody felt pretty fit, as the wines and liqueurs were marvellous. One of the pilots produced a fiddle, and another a saxophone, and a dance was started up. There were only about three ladies there—the French Consul's wife, the Commandant's wife, and another. They persuaded me into dressing up in my Roumanian costume. Combined with a pair of baggy Arab trousers, the result was startling if not exactly true to type. I then had to do a dance. It is curious how one can play the fool when with foreigners, whereas one can become so absolutely self-conscious and awkward with people of one's own nationality.

At long last my spares arrived from England. The Italians did all my repairs for me and refused to charge me a penny. After two Saints' Days, which are the equivalent to holidays there, had run their course, Elijah was once more ready to take the air. This was at 12 o'clock on Tuesday morning. I was really quite nervous about flying again. For one thing, I had not yet flown in Africa in daylight. Stories of the rarity of the atmosphere near the ground causing the kite to drop the last ten feet like a stone had put the wind up me. Apart from that, I had not flown since I had capoted; meanwhile, also, the machine had been repaired. On the whole I decided the sooner I got going the better for my peace of mind. The aerodrome officials did not like my going up, as there was rather a strong wind blowing. Finally it was arranged, and we wheeled the machine out into the sand-laden air. It is always a marvel to me that the carburettor does not choke up with such quantities of sand blown into it.

I found my first sight of Africa from the air most interesting. The sea was bluer than I had ever seen it before; there was the salt pan in which I had capoted, and away to the south my first glimpse of the Desert, which looked like brown liquid that had overflowed from some source beyond the horizon. Everything looked quite different from the picture which I had built up in my imagination. However, it was not the time for sight-seeing, and, as I felt decidedly uncomfortable in the aeroplane, I thought I had better get on to the business. First of all I did a couple of stall turns and then I went into a loop. I looped down the wind, which I think is a mistake. Anyway, when Elijah got into a vertical position there she stuck. Visions of torn elevators in a tail slide made me keep the controls as steady as I could; she seemed to stand on her tail for an interminable time, until I began to wonder what was going to happen. Finally she fell over slowly backwards. On the whole it was the worst loop I have ever done, and nothing soothing about it for the nerves either. After doing one or two more I had a shot at a spin. When I set about coming out of it nothing happened. I thought, " Here is the end of the penny section." However, the old brain must have brightened up a bit then, because presently we struggled out of it, and went into a dive at 130 miles an hour. The fact of the matter was, I was flying in the world's worst fashion.

After another spin—a little better this time—the next thing on the programme was to land. I had to land across a narrow part of the aerodrome. The distance between the hangars and the drains being dug on the aerodrome was about 275 yards. This was where I should have landed the night I capoted. Under ordinary circumstances this distance would give plenty of room, but on this occasion I would have liked three times as much. I wanted to land faster for fear of the ten foot pancake. On the first attempt I overshot, so I pretended I had only come down to look at the aerodrome and went off again. The whole staff had turned out to watch the fun, which was not calculated to improve my performance. Next time I slipped between the hangars, the hangar roofs being above me on either wing-tip; but I was so busy watching the tree-tops, the telegraph wires, and the hangar-tops, that I bumped hard. One thing about frequently making bad landings is that you know more or less what to do; I put the engine on full throttle and went off. The next shot I got down all right. The old " kite " got well shaken up, as the surface was pretty rough. All the staff swarmed round me like ants. I imagined they had come to see if I were still in one piece, and consequently felt an awful mutt. Judge of my astonishment then, when Ghirlando told me that the Italian mechanics said I had given a most excellent exhibition of stunting. I could not help laughing, knowing I had made the world's worst exhibition. Apparently, the Italians don't stunt much, or the mechanics would be able to distinguish between good and bad work. Of course, when you come to think of it, that stalled loop may have seemed quite spectacular from the ground, and perhaps they could not tell that I only got down by the skin of my teeth.

There was an almost daily incident which grew rather to amuse me. I think every pilot at the 'drome approached me at one time or another and conducted a conversation on the following lines :—

" What is your final destination? " he would ask.

" Sydney."

" That is in Australia, is it not? "

" Yes."

" How much farther is it from here? "

" 13,000 miles."

" What does that make in kilometres? "

" 20,800 kilometres."

Then he would walk away shaking his head slowly and muttering :

" It is a long way."

CHAPTER VII

ON January the seventh Ghirlando helped me to replenish my larder. I bought dates, biscuits, cheese, fruit, nuts, sardines, tinned fish, tinned meat, chocolate, tinned fruit, not to mention a litre of wine for myself, and another for dedication to Minerva in Sydney, if the journey should ever come to a safe ending. In addition I decided that immediate propitiation was also necessary. But wine was not strong enough for the task: I bought some of the finest brandy I could find.

On January the eighth Elijah was once more ready for action, and I packed all my gear back into her. The prospect of starting off again for home was quite exciting. I wanted to have another practice flight, but it could not be arranged. Either the wind was—in the opinion of the aerodrome authorities—too strong, or else the Doctor was not present. What with the accidents to Jones-Williams, to Lasalle, to André, to their own Romeo and to me all occurring in that part of the world the same week, they were getting a bit breezy lest there should be any more.

Next morning I was up before dawn, bursting to start again. I looked at the wind. It blew with some force from the S.W. Nothing could have suited me better. The night duty officer said he hadn't slept a wink, he was worried about having to see me safely away. I could not feel properly sympathetic, having myself slept like a log. He said he must have a weather report before I left. A mechanic and I got Elijah ready and pushed her out of the hangar in the dark with the aid of some Arabs. Standing squarely in front, I smashed the cognac on the propeller boss. The fumes rose strongly and pungently from the sand. I felt the voyage would start well. I started up the motor, then waited impatiently for the weather report. Dawn had just broken when the duty pilot arrived at the double to say the weather conditions at Syrte were absolutely prohibitive: a sand storm of such and such velocity. I cussed hard. The weather was good at Tripoli; if it was too bad when I reached Syrte, I could either land or come back. I went back to my room and had another snooze. At half-past eight the weather at Tripoli was perfect, so I begged them to get another report from Syrte. The answer came back that conditions were improving. After some hesitation they said I could leave. I was in the air fifteen minutes from their giving the word.

It was a great feeling to find myself scudding over the desert homewards. We battled along at over 100 m.p.h. with a strong sou'-westerly wind. The short run to Homs was very interesting. I tried to associate my present impressions of this stretch with the impressions I had formed during the trip by night, but that proved impossible, for it all looked entirely different. It was a good job I had not tried landing on the beach between Homs and Tripoli. There was only about ten yards between the edge of the sea and a low cliff. In the middle of the ten yards strip ran a six to ten foot wall of solidly packed dead seaweed. The jetty at Homs alone was recognisable. The aerodrome there looked big and easy. I wondered what would have happened had I tried to land there that night. The village of mud houses did not look very thrilling.

Visibility was excellent. Lovely deep blue fringe to the ocean. On the coast occasional patches of vineyards and olive groves with few trees, otherwise the brown desert stretching to the southern horizon. The colour seemed about the same as that with which the desert is usually marked in atlases. Between Misurata at the 140 mile mark to Syrte at the 265 mile mark I do not recall seeing a single house. The string of handsome-looking names shown on the map only indicate water-wells. We had left Tripoli at 9.18 and hit Syrte at 11.55. I kept a look-out for the remains of Lasalle's machine, but did not see anything. The country was now good flying country. The sea shore had broadened and flattened out; even inland it looked as if a forced landing could be made almost anywhere with comparative safety. I may say flying was now a comfortable operation compared to the London-Tripoli run.

After the dozen mud houses of Syrte, nothing of interest occurred till we had turned the gulf of Syrte and headed north. At el Agheila, 500 miles from Tripoli, the air thickened and the wind increased in force to some 50 miles an hour, blowing from the south-east. We sailed along with a drift to port of 358. The air got thicker and thicker until we were forced down to within 200 feet of the ground, and even then I could see only a small patch of ground directly beneath the plane. Nothing was visible even a few hundred yards ahead. I considered turning back to Syrte, having heard of sand storms the thickness of pea soup (although I'll guarantee I have eaten pea soups thicker than any sand storm ever made). In the end I decided to carry on till we ran into the pea soup variety. Just before meeting this sand storm, flying along in perfect weather above easy terrain, the thought of a flying accident had seemed ludicrous; now nothing seemed more likely. Strike this in the dark—and you might run into it with absolute suddenness as into a brick wall—and what chance would a pilot have if he tried to keep sight of the earth all the time? Fortunately it grew no thicker, and at Ghemines we ran out of it again.

Benghazi soon showed up—a solid pack of buildings on the edge of the sea—with the sun shining full on the white houses. We landed at 3.30 to find the British Pro-Consul waiting for our arrival. Thanks to the powerful wind we had cut out the 610 miles in 6 hours 12 minutes.

I had a most enjoyable evening with Mr. Chaffy, the British Consul, André the Swedish pilot, and a local farmer named Bazzan. Had it been twice as long the evening would have been all too short. That is the worst part about long flights. If you weren't making the flight you would not meet the interesting people you do. But if you stay and talk to the interesting people you can't make the flight. Chaffy talked about Marlborough College to me, for we had both been there. There are generally a few yarns to swap with one's old school-fellows. As for André—put two airmen together any time, anywhere, and shop and gossip will flow ad. lib. till further orders. André had made a flight to the Cape from Sweden in his Cirrus Moth and was now on his way home again. He had the usual 3½-4 hours' range with his bus, so goodness only knows how many landings he had made. He had wrecked his machine south of Ghemines a few days previously. He had started off for Tripoli, but south of Ghemines ran into a sand storm. His visibility became so bad that he decided to land, and made a good landing on some firm sand a few hundred yards from the sea. All went well for an hour or two, until the wind began to increase in strength. At dusk he went out and was compelled to hang on to one wing to prevent the machine being blown over. He held on till after midnight, every now and then being lifted off the ground, but managed to prevent the machine from being blown over. Presently, however, to his astonishment water began lapping his ankles. In almost no time it was up to his knees. Then the tail of the machine was covered, and still the water was rising. It crept up past his waist, until the lower wings of the machine were completely under water. André stuck to his job until finally he had to swim ashore, leaving the plane with its upper wings and nose sticking out of the water, and a very sad sight it must have been too. Apparently the sea had broken through the sand bank separating the shore from where he was. André had no food or water. The only thing to do was to set off for the nearest town, which, if I remember rightly, was Syrte. For $2\frac{1}{2}$ days he tramped on, eventually arriving at Syrte half dead from hunger and thirst. From there he was driven back to Benghazi by motor, and the Italians sent out a truck to collect the aeroplane. The aeroplane was all right, only full of salt water. They loaded it on to the truck, and all would have been well had not the Italians been in an urgent hurry to return to Benghazi before dark for fear they should be caught by the Arabs. First of all a jolt sent the plane banging into the front of the truck and broke the propeller. Then another jolt snapped the tail off on the end of the truck, and as far as I can make out, there was not much aeroplane left by the time they reached Benghazi.

Bazzan told us about his farm life and drew me a little map to show where the farm was. It is not far from Benghazi, and consists of a square-built house in the middle of some 10,000 acres of ground which he owns. Judging from the air, one would not think it worth while to own 10,000,000 acres in that part of the world. However, he says he grows olives and grapes. When the day's work is done, he and his henchmen retire into the house and everyone sleeps soundly except the four men who man the four machine guns, one in each corner of the house. I used to think farming was rather too quiet a game, but maybe under these circumstances it would be more interesting. I was told there had been a bombing raid on some Arabs, ten miles out of Benghazi, only the day before. They tell unbelievably gruesome stories of what happens to aviators or other white men who fall into the Arabs' hands in that part of the world. The Commandant of the aerodrome was quite annoyed with me because I was not carrying a rifle. However, I had got an Arab acquaintance of mine in Tripoli to write on the back of my purse, in Arabic, to say that I was a British aviator and that we had been friends from our boyhood up, so to speak. On the strength of this, he adjured any Arab warriors who came in touch with me to do their best for me instead of worst, which is their usual practice.

Next morning, I was driven out to the aerodrome in the dark and left Benghazi at 6.35. The

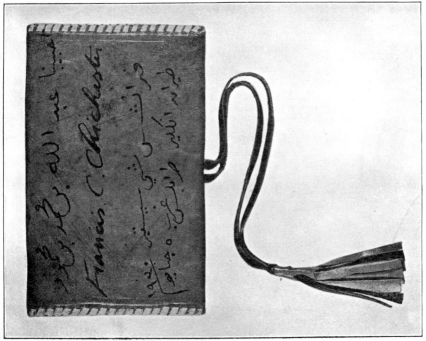

THE ARAB PURSE WITH INSCRIPTION

flat sandy stretches soon changed to steepish hills
extending sometimes to the water's edge. A strong
westerly wind drove us along at a good pace with
25º starboard drift. We reached Tolmetta in 43
minutes, about 75 miles. At Tolmetta the course
was changed to nearly due east, which put the
wind directly behind until we reached Derna.
Here it was necessary to change course again to
south-east. This put the wind on the other quarter,
so that now we were drifting nearly 25º to port.
We were crossing a high flat plateau, intersected
by deep narrow ravines running down to the coast.
It was ideal flying country; the weather was ideal;
the wind was ideal; in fact, everything in the
garden was lovely.

Three hours out from Benghazi we were a few
miles past Mersa-tobruk and had made 290 miles in
that time. Presently, at es-Sollum, at the 360 mile
peg, we crossed into British territory, and I presume it was only imagination which made the
terrain seem immediately more matter-of-fact and
less interesting. There was really not much to do
except eat, pump up petrol, and admire the scenery.
Some of the colours of the sea close to the shore
were marvellous, but there was nothing very wonderful about the dirty mud-coloured sand wastes
stretching as far as you could see inland.

I had advised the Egyptian authorities that I
was going to land at Mersa-Matruh. In Egypt
they are very strict. You must send forward
information the day before arriving, also details of
the machine and odds and ends of information
about yourself. When you arrive, you have to
clear the Medical-Customs-Police, as well as the
Aerodrome Authorities.

We reached Mersa-Matruh at 11.55, having

travelled 504 miles from Benghazi. I particularly wanted to reach Abu-sueir that night, to see my cousin, who is a pilot instructor there. This aerodrome is 350 miles further on. It was necessary to allow 4½ hours to reach it. In addition we were losing about an hour's daylight in the run from Benghazi to Abu-sueir. We must arrive at Abu-sueir by five o'clock. Therefore, if we stopped at Mersa-Matruh, from which place I felt sure we would not get away in less than two hours, it would be impossible to reach Abu-sueir that night. I calculated my petrol. I had only been 5 hours 20 minutes in the air so far, and although I had not filled up my No. 2 tank at Benghazi, I felt confident that I had enough petrol to reach Abu-sueir. I decided not to leave my card with the Egyptian Authorities at Mersa-Matruh, and pushed straight on for Abu-sueir.

As far as I was concerned, the rest of the day's journey was not amusing. Everything ceases to be amusing after six hours in an open plane. By then the engine beat has drummed itself into every nerve of your body. You find yourself squirming every few minutes to try and find a fresh part of your anatomy to sit on. It takes an hour and twenty minutes to pump both the lower tanks of petrol up to the top tank, and as you must keep your feet steady on the rudder-bars meanwhile, the restricted movement of your muscles when carrying out this work induces after a time considerable soreness bordering on cramp. During the first few hours in the air you have a hearty appetite, and already that day I had made serious inroads into the 2½ kilograms of dates I carried, as well as sampling the biscuits and cheese, sardines, and tinned fruit. But by now my appetite had gone and I could not be bothered to eat any more. As for scenery, there is such a vast stretch of country to be seen from a plane that after a while it is almost necessary not to look at it, your brain gets fatigued taking in so much. Imagine climbing a 4,000 foot mountain and admiring the view for six or seven hours on end. You can admire the scenery at the beginning of the day's flight, but after that it is the interest and excitement of the unknown which supplies zest to the trip. The fact of not knowing what is going to turn up behind the next chain of mountains; of wondering what sort of an aerodrome you are coming to; of thinking what the weather is going to be like. Another great satisfaction is the feeling of cutting out the distance. It tickles the vanity of man to think that he, more or less of his sole volition, is hourly some eighty miles nearer a goal originally fourteen or fifteen thousand miles away. Perhaps that is why a little favourable wind makes such a great difference to the pleasure of the day's flying. It must be only imagination which induces a certain feeling of contentment if the speed is exceeding 80 m.p.h. even if it be only by 5 m.p.h., whereas a mere 5 m.p.h. off the 80 induces a corresponding feeling of discontentment.

By 12 o'clock the wind had dropped to nothing. After turning the foot of the gulf west of Alexandria it seemed an interminable time till we left the desert at the beginning of the Nile Delta. To make it worse, my engine seemed to be changing its note. There was very little difference, but when you sit behind a motor for many hours listening intently to its tune, you become extraordinarily sensitive to the slightest change. There was not enough to worry about seriously, but it

91

indicated the possibility of trouble in the near future.

A more boring country than the Nile Delta, seen from the air, it is difficult to imagine. It seems to represent life at its dullest and deadliest. It is all sliced up into countless tiny allotments. You feel mean to be up in the air, free, and with great space at your command, while down below all these people are born, toil and die on their patches of a few square yards. Anyway it is remarkably unpleasant country for forced landings, and something of the monotony of existence which you feel must be the key-note of the inhabitants' lives seems to communicate itself to you up above. I always had romantic notions about Egypt, but the sight of the villages and towns with their thousands of mud shacks jammed together quickly dispelled them. It was very pleasing when the desert reappeared and gave the impression that the sand, like a vast flow of lava, was invading the fertile country we had been flying over.

As we we nearing Abu-sueir, we passed over some lines of trenches dug in the sand on the north side of the railway line. I thought this was a very exposed spot to dig trenches. What a perfect mark they seemed to offer to modern artillery! Later on, I inquired about them, and was told they were not built for the last war, but that I had been looking at the old battlefield of Tel-el-Kebir, and that they were not really trenches, but raised mounds, used on the memorable occasion of that battle.

When quite close to Abu-sueir, I saw a tall column of black smoke rising from the aerodrome. I thought my cousin had seen me coming, and was being facetious, by building an unnecessarily huge

92

smoke signal for my benefit. As a matter of fact, the true cause of that smoke was anything but comic. They were burning the debris of the planes which had collided two days previously and been smashed to smithereens, killing four pilots.

We landed at Abu-sueir at 3.50, after a non-stop run of 854 miles, which had taken 9 hours 15 minutes. I taxied up to the hangars. A small crowd of men stood some thirty yards away, and just stared as one can imagine Aborigines staring at the first white man they had ever seen. This was an unwelcome change from the custom of the Italians, who invariably send out their duty officer to inquire solicitously who you are and how you are. In the end I went over and persuaded somebody to hunt up my cousin.

Civil planes are not supposed to land at Abu-sueir. When my cousin directed his squad to give me a hand with the machine, they thought the Moth was a colossal joke. They had been stationed out there for some years and had never seen a baby machine before. As soon as I got a chance I tried the compression of all cylinders and found No. 2 cylinder reading from the front was blowing slightly through the exhaust valve. It was not particularly serious, but it foreboded trouble sooner or later. The idea of having to dismantle the engine was unpleasant. I hoped it would see me through to Karachi.

My cousin took me off and introduced me to the mess, where I had some lengthy glasses of beer. It was wonderful stuff; unfortunately after some time in the air one drink is enough to put you " on one ear " so to speak. The officers were discussing the duck-shoot from which they had just returned. I found the idea of shooting duck in Egypt very

93

surprising.   Actually, I believe they get great sport from it.

I had a bit of a yarn with my cousin and was about to turn in when the Duty Pilot arrived.   He had just received orders from Cairo to say that as I had failed to clear Customs at Mersa-Matruh or Cairo, I must return immediately to Heliopolis, the aerodrome of Cairo, in order to go through the necessary formalities.   I replied " Hm," which was really all there was to say.   To reach Heliopolis meant returning 65 miles towards England.

CHAPTER VIII

Next morning I got up at dawn after an excellent sleep in my cousin's room.

On reaching the hangar the first thing I did was to try the compression again. With the engine cold, that valve was rotten. I felt anxious about it and sadly regretted not having checked the clearances after the tappets had been adjusted by the Italian mechanic at Tripoli. My cousin suggested having it fixed, but I did not like losing daylight if it could possibly be avoided. In the end I decided to try and finish another day's run before fixing it.

Before I left, the Duty Pilot arrived with the order for me to return to Cairo. I had to sign this to show it had reached me.

We got away at 6.53 and I turned Elijah's nose towards Cairo. But I think Elijah had her own prejudices in the matter. Perhaps she thought that where Moses had gone, Elijah should follow. At any rate, instead of arriving at Cairo, I presently found to my astonishment that Elijah was taking me over the Red Sea (Suez Canal) towards Jerusalem.

Crossing the Canal was interesting. I was sorry there was no ship in sight. It must be a great sight to see one ploughing through the sand. The desert on either side of the Canal was of the real nothing-but-sand variety. Seen from 4,000 feet altitude it exactly resembled the sand on a sheltered piece of shore worked into sills and wavelets by the receding tide. If there were not a few palm trees sticking through the sand here and there near the coast, I think it would be difficult to judge one's height above those sand dunes. I felt strong sympathy for Moses when I thought I was covering in 40 minutes the distance over which he had taken 40 years.

I rather went to sleep following the coast. I had been informed in England that there was a landing ground at Rafa, so when we presently came across one I put it down as Rafa. Then the thought entered my head that it was much too good a landing ground for Rafa, so I investigated closely and found the name Gaza written across it. Here I was due to re-fuel. On landing I asked them about Rafa, which is 16 miles to the south-west, but they stated they had never heard of a landing ground there. Gaza is an Imperial Airways aerodrome—the first I had come across. They were out to help me in every way they could, and in most hospitable fashion, just as afterwards at all the aerodromes of this company which I came across.

On testing No. 2 cylinder again I found it was pretty bad. Not only would it not carry me to Karachi, it must be fixed that night at the latest. This was a confounded nuisance; grinding in valves without tools is no fun at the best of times. I consulted Mr. Brackley, of Imperial Airways, who happened to be at Gaza. He recommended my stopping at Rutba Wells. Imperial Airways had a mechanic stationed there, who would help me. I asked him a lot of questions about the desert. He said I would have to keep my eyes skinned sometimes to follow the tracks.

I tucked some wonderful eggs under my wing, and after re-fuelling left again at 10.25. We started climbing immediately. The rough-looking hills between Hebron and Jerusalem were very forbidding; I had been warned that the bumps are exceedingly bad thereabouts. The hills are just over 3,000 feet high, so I climbed up to 5,000. One advantage of being scared of something is that it frequently does not eventuate; in this case there was hardly a bump.

Imagine how interesting it was passing over this country. To the north, nestling on the bald tops of the hill-chain running north and south, was Hebron. Quite a number of roads spread across the flats and wound among the hills. The whole country looked very bare, as if a giant wave had swept over it and washed out by the roots anything green; perhaps it looks more fertile in summer. But it did not seem right that a country which had been fought over and fought for such countless times should be anything but a green and smiling land. Ahead lay the Dead Sea, not a movement stirring its surface, bedded deeply in the hill land.

I am sorry to say I made a bad mistake in navigation, although I am still at a loss to understand how I did it. When I arrived at the Dead Sea I was eighteen miles south of where I should have been. It did not make much difference there, but it gives you a shock when you find you can make a mistake like that, especially as after the Dead Sea the pukka desert starts and there are few, if any, easily distinguishable landmarks. Here the same error would be a pretty serious affair. I flew north up the Dead Sea until I came to where I should have been earlier, and then continued on my course. Now the country seemed to be all mud

97

and sand. Where by the map one expected to find a big town, only a collection of a few mud houses eventuated. It was a relief to pick up Ziza, which lies in a long, deep, but smooth valley of light-brown colour stretching out of sight north and south, with the railway line running up it. There were only two or three shacks there, but the scars made by aeroplane tail-skids were visible on the landing ground behind the houses.

I altered course to 84° and headed into the genuine article in deserts. No doubt one gets far more sport out of the first trip across the desert than one is likely to get on any subsequent occasion. I had definite enough information about what to expect, namely that there would be the wheel tracks of the convoy which had motored through. These would be visible most of the time. Also there were furrows ploughed in the sand here and there, now on one side of the track, now on the other. These had been put in for guidance. Finally there were landing grounds at various spots averaging about 20 miles apart, and marked with letters of the alphabet. This information happened to be perfectly correct. Unfortunately you get so much untrustworthy and often definitely incorrect information that you end up by never trusting any. Then, in addition, a description by someone else frequently paints in your brain a picture different to that intended.

Altogether, I did not know what on earth to expect should I have difficulty in discovering the track. Were there others beside the main track? Should I have difficulty in differentiating these others from the main track? Could I rely on the funny-looking map which I had for this crossing? It looked so very haphazard, with bits of hills

98

marked in here and there near the track, but with nothing at all shown ten miles to the north or south.

I looked all round. There was nothing in sight north, south, east or west, but brown sand and a few hills far away on the northern horizon.

The track comes down from Amman to the north. We should strike it 20 miles after leaving Gaza. I watched the ground as never before. We covered the 20 miles without a sign of it, only the bare illimitable sand stretching out of sight without a trace of humanity.

This was disturbing, especially as it followed so close upon the error I had made after leaving Gaza.

Twenty-five miles slipped by; and as we covered mile after mile without signs of anything, I grew more anxious until, 33 miles from Ziza, I began to think I must turn back and start afresh; then suddenly away on my left I spotted a square building on the side of a rise. I turned immediately and crossed to it. It stood like a solid block of stone—no windows or doors as far as I could see. I circled it, and behind the house on top of the rise found the groove made in the sand by aeroplane tail-skids. Good!

I hunted for a letter " C " which ought to identify the first landing ground according to my information, but there was none to be seen. I was puzzled. Why the tail-skid marks and yet no letter? I searched for a track and to my great joy spotted the two wheel tracks, which I followed immediately, still feeling rather puzzled. " C," the first landing ground shown on the map, was on the N.E. corner of what appeared to be either a lake or a marsh. There was no lake or marsh here, yet that might signify little, for my map looked capable of anything. However, " C " was supposed to be 50 miles from Ziza, and I felt sure we had not covered that distance. Nevertheless there undoubtedly was the track, and running more or less in the right direction.

The next ground should now be " D " at the 73 mile peg. 40 miles, 50, 60—this track was devilish hard to follow at times; we twisted and turned all over the place, but I stuck like a leech, scared of losing sight of it for a moment. 70, 75, 80 miles —not a trace of any landing ground. Whew! this was hot work! 85 miles, still no sign. I must try and get a check of our course by compass bearing. This was not so easy to do: for one thing we were drifting hard aport because of the strong southerly wind on our starboard beam, and for another, owing to the twisting and tortuous path we were following, the compass needle was swinging through a wide angle. I hated taking my eyes off those two faint wheel marks for a second, but it was the only thing to do. I compromised by darting a look at the compass, then at the ground, and so on. The compass needle seemed to be swinging between about $80°$ and $140°$, so I split the difference and decided we were travelling on about $110°$. Hades! we should be on $84°$! "Cuss it," I thought, "this confounded compass has gone wrong." Then I recalled the dozens of occasions upon which I had argued with my compass, only to lose the argument every time; until finally I had been forced to adopt an axiom that "good compasses never lie." "Good Lord," I said to myself, " I'm probably headed for Mecca. This is no good to me! " Now I must keep cool, a desert was no place to lose one's head. Let me

100

reason things out. First of all, I would trust my compass. We were now 90 miles from Ziza. That mud building with the tail-skid marks near by must have been on the main route. I must have been on the right track at that point. All right, let me mark the main track at the 33 mile peg and then plot a point 57 miles farther on, on a bearing of 110° That took me to a point 30 miles south of the route. Now, what should I do? Well, there was only one correct course to adopt; we must retrace our path and start afresh. On the other hand, turning back is a pestilential proceeding; and again, my compass had not yet been proved wrong, that main track ought to be 30 miles to the north. Finally, the excitement of cutting over the unmapped open desert was irresistible. I headed Elijah due north, dropping down close to the ground and watching it as never before; I think I would have seen a rat on it. But of course I hadn't come across a living thing, animal or vegetable, since leaving Ziza.

Immediately we left the track we had been on, the vibration caused by the ill-running motor seemed to increase threefold, and I was painfully aware of it all the time in spite of telling myself it was only imagination. We scudded along at a fast pace with the strong wind behind us, yet every mile we covered seemed to take an age. Not only that, but I seemed to be aware of every inch of ground crossed: dry depressions, dry watercourses, dirty black hills. On the flats the surface seemed to be all sandy mud, dull, bare, lifeless.

It was exciting, that run across the desert; what a king of sports!

Twenty-five miles from the old track we should be on the borders of the mapped country

101

if my calculations were correct—26 miles.

We came to a pass in a chain of hills. A dried-up water-course ran through it and on the north side split into three. These hills looked like those marked on the map as Jebel Tibish. If so, the track should turn up in two or three minutes. I redoubled my look-out, darting a glance now on this side, now on that, and even turning constantly to look back at the hills to see if they still resembled the Tibish. Then suddenly, there was the track, quite different this time. Where it crossed a dried-up water-course not two but several wheel ruts showed clearly. Compared to the one I had previously been on, it was like a city thoroughfare. There was much rejoicing in the air. Even so I would take no chances. I wanted to see with my own eyes this " D " landing ground, so turned back towards Ziza. If we were where calculated, " D " should appear in a few minutes. At one o'clock it came into sight. There were the tail-skid marks, and—ha !—there was the letter " D " marked on the ground. I promptly turned right about and set sail again, singing to myself a little song about an old friend of mine called " Antonio."

No work has to be done in preparing these landing grounds. Naturally suitable spots have been selected, then marked with letters of the alphabet. After I had struck D, it was fairly easy following the track, because in most places where there might have been some difficulty, arrows pointing out the right direction had been marked on the ground. You must never take your eyes off the track for more than a few moments; it twists and turns all over the place. The country is mostly of an undulating nature, and appears exactly the same type as Australian sheep country,

102

except that there does not seem to be the slightest sign of any vegetation. Two human heads which have a pretty close resemblance in shape look very different when one is covered with a luxuriant growth of hair, while the other is of a shiny baldness. The amazing thing is suddenly to come upon an Arab caravan, with a flock of sheep. How they exist it is impossible to imagine. I came across the first of these about 200 miles from Ziza. Till then there had been no sign of human, animal, or vegetable life.

I got more enjoyment out of crossing this stretch of country than I had yet obtained over any other part of the route. As soon as you get into the desert, an extraordinary sense of freedom gives you a feeling of well-being. It is rather depressing flying over Europe, where every inch of ground is occupied, and even the Alps are criss-crossed in all directions with footpaths.

Later in the afternoon, it became very difficult to pick up the track, because the sun getting low made it hard to distinguish the two ruts from the surrounding country. I had been flying all day at an altitude of 4,000 feet. Looking down at the ground, I began in a sleepy fashion to think that the altimeter must be wrong. Presently, however, it dawned on me that we were now passing over country which, although comparatively flat on the surface, was up to 3,000 feet above sea level. My log book has notes of passing the following landing grounds :—

J, 1.45 p.m.
L, 1.58 p.m.
N, 2.17 p.m.
O, 2.27 p.m.
Rutba Wells, 3.23 p.m.   Day's run 582 miles.

CHAPTER IX

I was extraordinarily intrigued by the whole outfit at Rutba Wells. In the first place, it was fun landing on the desert, and then, what an interesting spot. There were camel caravans there. It is a stopping place also for the motor caravans which run from Baghdad to Damascus. These are owned by Nairn Brothers, who are New Zealanders. There was a squad of Iraquian infantry, gentlemen of an appearance half Indian and half European. Here also, the Imperial Airways machines spend the night; altogether a most interesting spot. The track I had been following from Palestine is rarely if ever used, but at Rutba Wells you strike the main track to Damascus from Baghdad. Imperial Airways have a mechanic stationed there. I told him I wanted to grind my valves in, and asked him to give me a hand. He was not very keen at first; it meant working into the night. Also, he had only worked on one type of engine, and was a little nervous about handling a Gypsy. But the work had to be done; I couldn't go on with the machine vibrating as it had been. I said I would show him how to work everything. We pushed Elijah through the barbed wire entanglements enclosing the square stone building, which was really a fort. We drew her up to the window of the mechanic's room, and I left him to take off the intake mani-

104

fold, while I had a snooze. They stuck me into a room with the Iraquian officer; I was just getting off to sleep when he entered, shuffled up and down the room, sniffed and snorted. Each time I was on the point of dozing off he sniffed or he snorted; and each time he sniffed or snorted I got more peeved, as it spoilt my chance of a little badly needed sleep. He asked me a few silly questions in French. Of course, time means little or nothing to people living out there; they cannot understand anybody finding such an absurdly small unit of time as an hour or a day of any value.

I could see no chance of getting any sleep, so I finally went off in disgust to give the mechanic a hand. We got off the manifold and piston head. The exhaust valve was badly fitted; I produced a new one, as I thought it would take less time to grind in. The mechanic had an electric light extension which he fastened to the pendant in his room, led through the window, and fastened on to the tip of the propeller blade. It began to freeze. We finished the grinding and put the cylinder back. I said:

"Let's test it before we put the manifold on."

When we came to test it, it was worse than before. This set us both thinking furiously. By all the rules it should be perfect, for we had done everything as it should be done. For a moment I was undecided whether to take it down again or to finish reassembling, in the hope that it would settle into place when the motor was started. It was getting late and I was extremely tired; however, in the end I decided we had better take it off. Then we took the valves out again and looked at them. They certainly looked and seemed all right. We fitted them back into the cylinder head and filled it up with petrol before completing the assembly. It held the petrol; it simply must be all right, so we fitted it on to the engine, and this time it was. The first time a piece of dirt must have got on to the valve seating. It was 11.30 before we finished the job.

When I got to bed I lay for a while listening to some delightful music. It sounded like music from flutes, quietly tinkling bells, and perhaps a few outlandish instruments I had not heard before.

Got up as usual at five o'clock next morning and ate a cold sand grouse as I dressed. The manager of the place, Mr. Fraser, had made me a present of two that he had shot the day before. I asked whence had come the music I had listened to overnight. " Music! " he said, " impossible! the vibration of the motor must have affected the nerves of your ear-drums."

When it came to starting Elijah up again, there was nothing doing. It was exceedingly cold, we took it in turns pulling the prop round, and both got worn out at it. It would fire once, but would not have enough power to overcome the next compression. This was caused by the cold; it had frozen during the night, which surprised me, as I had always thought the Arabian desert to be a particularly hot spot. I happened to look at the oil gauge at one point, and noticed that with our manual efforts we had got the pressure up to 40 pounds per square inch. At last, in desperation I sent the mechanic off to get some hot water, in the hopes that mixing a little with the petrol would make it more explosive. No sooner had he gone than Elijah went off with a roar. I took off at 7.35 feeling quite exhausted. The oil pressure dropped to 15 pounds to the square inch, and it put

106

the breeze up me. However, I did not land again immediately, thinking that it might be a natural consequence of the cold, although I could not quite understand it, as you would think the pressure would mount in cold weather, instead of dropping. If it did not mount, why had it gone up to 40 pounds to the square inch through our turning of the air screw? I flew dead slow for ten minutes— pressure increased to 20 pounds to the square inch. This lessened my anxiety, and I gradually speeded up as the oil pressure slowly climbed to its normal 45 pounds to the square inch.

The desert was magnificent in the early morning sun. I have seldom enjoyed a flight more. The road was now comparatively crowded, for I saw two motor cars in the first hundred miles, also several Arab caravans encamped in black tents, some with flocks of sheep. The weather was absolutely perfect. As usual, on these perfect days, when flying is so easy, I rather went to sleep, and happening to look to my left, I spotted, three or four miles away, a large city which I had almost passed. "Whatever is that?" I thought, and searched my map. It was Baghdad, so I hopped across. I had been warned that there had been a lot of rain, and that the aerodrome might be dangerous. It looked horrid from the air, like a big mud-flat. However, when I flew low over the surface I could not see any traces of anything having sunk into the mud. I could therefore only infer that it was solid. I landed, and as a matter of fact it was as hard as a brick. The manager there, Mr. Phelps, was the most efficient aerodrome official I have ever come across. He had the Medical, the Customs, and the Police authorities all waiting for me; he fed me; arranged the re-fuelling with 43 gallons of petrol and two gallons of oil; wrote his name on Elijah; and got me into the air again; all within fifty minutes. I told Mr. Phelps that I should have been along three weeks before if he had had a double in charge of each of the aerodromes I had stopped at en route.

Just after I had left the ground the engine cowling flew open. I had neglected to fasten it properly after inspecting the tappets. Fortunately I had taxied right to the end of the aerodrome before taking off, and I was able to land at the other end of the aerodrome without turning. Considering that I had 59 gallons of petrol on board, besides all the gear that I was carrying, I was astonished to find how easy it was to land with this load.

Mr. Phelps had also procured me a weather report. At ground level there was no wind, but the report said that the wind increased in force up to 5,000 feet, where it was blowing 35 miles an hour. So up I went straight away, and presently we were knocking out 104 miles an hour. At this height flying is not nearly so amusing, you lose a lot of detail of the country. The weather was perfect, there was not a movement in the air, and I got rather bored.

A few hours later we crossed into Persia. Here, the country took on a poverty-stricken look. It reminded me of a cockerel which had been in a fight and lost all its feathers. Not a sign of anything growing anywhere. Expanses of mud stretched away from the sea to the mountains. A few dirty-looking villages could be seen here and there, but it looked from the air as if it would be necessary to remain cooped inside them all the winter; anybody trying to walk about the country

108

GOVERNMENT OF 'IRAQ.
MINISTRY OF INTERIOR,
PUBLIC HEALTH DIRECTORATE,
BAGHDAD

حكومة العراق
وزارة الداخلية
مديرية الصحة
بغداد

No. _10/1/Private_

Date _12/1/30_

BILL OF HEALTH.

Certified that the aircraft _G-AAKK_

belonging to the _____ and under
the command of _Mr. Chichester_

bound for _New Zealand_ with a crew (including
Officer and all Staff) of _____

persons and _____ passengers, carrying a

cargo of _personal baggage_

is to-day the _Twelfth_ of _February_ 1930. at the

time of leaving the aerodrome of _Baghdad_ in

a satisfactory sanitary condition and that no case of infectious disease exists among its
passengers and crew.

Certified also that the City _of Baghdad_ is at present :—

(a) Free from Cholera, ~~Plague, Small-pox~~, Yellow fever or Typhus fever.

	Cholera,	Plague.	Small pox.	Yellow fever.	Typhus fever
Date of last case of	22/12/27	8/1/30	9/1/30	—	9/2/28

(b Infected with ~~Cholera~~, Plague, Small-pox, ~~Yellow fever, or Typhus~~ to the following
extent :—

	Cholera.	Plague.	Small pox.	Yellow fever.	Typhus fever.
Cases reported during week previous to sailing	—	1	1	—	—

HEALTH OFFICER,

Baghdad Station.

Facing page 108

would get drowned almost immediately in a sea of mud.

It was just getting dark when we reached Bushire. I passed over the lighted town, looking for the aerodrome. To come upon a town all lighted up and in a strange country has not, I find, a soothing effect on an airman. He thinks: " Is it possible there has been a mistake and there is no aerodrome here? If so, with darkness falling I am going to be in the soup." However, I discovered this aerodrome all right, by spotting a hangar. On close investigation I unearthed, so to speak, the flying field itself. It is bordered by white pylons. In the centre was a largish lake, and the ground not under water looked to be partly a bog and partly bumpy-looking terrain covered with marram grass. Right across the middle of the aerodrome was sauntering a motor car. As I flew over it to investigate the terrain, for I was in a hurry (it was now almost dark), the car stopped and disgorged two or three women, who fled for their lives in different directions, leaving the car stranded. Had I been actually landing, as they thought, I should surely have bowled over one of them.

I landed and taxied over towards the hangars. It was 5.10, the day's run had been 828 miles. As I switched off the engine my alarm clock went off. The Imperial Airways mechanic was greatly intrigued and asked me to explain the clock; I replied that as I was not as a rule much good at landing an aeroplane, I found an alarm clock of great use; it warned me when the time came for me to flatten out. In this case it must have made a mistake and gone off three minutes too late. The way I got this clock is rather curious. I realised that

109

one must have a good clock for cross-country work, so I made inquiries, and found that the aviation clock which I wanted would cost me £12 8s. 6d. Having a bad attack of unfinancialitis, I decided to save the £12, and paid 8/6 for a luminous-dialled alarm clock, constructed by Mr. Westclocks or Mr. Swiss, who make so many clocks. I stuck it between the telephone tube and the throttle rod, and I do not think it ever missed a beat.

After a short snooze, I went off to the sea shore and splashed about in the sea water, the world's best nerve tonic. It was a clear moonlight night. From where I sat, I noticed what I took to be two goats, solemnly watching me, as they stood on the end of a large log. They remained absolutely motionless, so that I got quite curious to find out why. Having dried myself by a run up and down the beach, I dressed and went over to investigate. What I thought were goats were the two wheels and under-carriage of a D.H. 9 A aeroplane carcass lying on its back and dripping petrol all over the place. It seemed rather a shame to waste it, so I filled my cigarette lighter from it, and went off to make inquiries as to its history. It appears that a Persian military pilot was flying this machine an hour or so before I arrived. He was flying badly, and ended up by flying bang into the top of the wireless mast. The result was that his propeller chewed in pieces the top of the mast and all the wires connected with it, thereby giving his aeroplane free passage. Then he made an excellent attempt to land the machine, and probably would have, had he been taking off into wind instead of down wind. The terrain ran a bit short; he somersaulted over the bank on to the sea shore, completely wrecking the machine, but escaping alive himself. He was miraculously fortunate in striking the top of the mast with the propeller, and thereby cutting all the wires. Had he hit it with his wing, or had he run into the wires between the poles, it would almost certainly have been the end of him.

The Imperial Airways mechanics here again did everything possible to help me. They also lent me an old camp bed; I spread my " flea bag," and after falling asleep to the same pretty tune played by my private orchestra, spent a most comfortable night in it until five o'clock, when the camp bed split in the middle, dropping me with a bump on to the floor.

I was up before dawn and left at daybreak: 6.15 by my clock. The morning was perfect, the sun at first barely shining through a rose-pink sky. The bay and mud-flats looked utterly calm and peaceful; here and there wreaths of mist floated above the water.

Thirty miles out we crossed over the Kuh-i-mund, a narrow ridge of hills formed like a fish's backbone, with countless limestone ridges of razor-back sharpness. These hills rise to a height of 3,200 feet. All the country along here is monotonous, composed of mud-flats, with these sharp, steep limestone hills rising suddenly out of them. I presume that in spring the mud is very fertile, but to look at it in winter you would think it was completely desert.

At the 260 mile peg, we passed abreast of Qais Island, which Marco Polo mentions in his travels, having made it a port of call in the year 1271 A.D. It was on the coast here that the pilots of an Imperial Airways machine had an unpleasant experience. Developing engine trouble they made an emergency landing with safety. One can picture the semi-barbarous Persian villagers swarming out to inspect this modern pterodactyl. Doubtless they imagined it a direct gift to them from heaven, or perhaps some of the harder cases of the village wished to display their prowess before the rest, for they advanced on the pilots and, pushing their gun-barrels into the pilots' stomachs, proceeded to strip them of all their clothing. At this moment, fortunately for the preservation of their under-pants, the mechanic who was working unseen on the recalcitrant motor suddenly got it to go. The pilots made a bolt for it, tumbled into the cabin, and off went the plane like a peppered cat. No doubt the astonished natives did pepper it too.

The weather was excellent all the morning, with not a movement in the air. Flying was as easy as A B C; in fact, I read an old newspaper that I had picked up at Bushire.

The log reads :—

" 1st hour—75 miles.
Height, 5,000 feet.
2nd hour—80 miles.
3rd hour—83 miles.
4th hour—89 miles.
5th hour—84 miles.
6th hour—92 miles.
Estimate Jask 12.55."

We landed at Jask at 12.55, after a 560 mile run. Jask is a splendid landing ground. The Imperial Airways staff gave me some bacon and eggs and tea, and we left 55 minutes later, after filling up with 36 gallons of petrol. I see a note in the log book that I was anxious about landing at Chahbar with an almost full load. Chahbar is only 200 miles from Jask. We landed there at

4.10, after a day's run of 760 miles. I was warmly greeted by Mr. Hackett, the only European there. He is in charge of the telegraph station. Quite a crowd of Persians turned out to look at the aeroplane, and a Persian military officer wrote his name on Elijah in Persian. An Indian working under Mr. Hackett asked permission to bring his womenfolk up. Apparently he must wait till everyone else had gone, as they were purdah, and not allowed to be seen by anybody.

The Persian military provided a guard for the night, and Mr. Hackett took me off to dinner. He was extraordinarily pleased to have a European visitor, the first he had seen for several months. Sir Alan Cobham had stopped here on his flight out. Mr. Hackett told me about Cobham's mechanic, Elliott, who was caught by a pot-shot from an Arab when crossing the desert. Rotten luck, as a plane takes a lot of hitting with a rifle.

I was just getting off to sleep about 11 o'clock when a gust of wind blew round the house. I hopped out of bed, put on the Sidcote suit over my pyjamas, and went out to the aeroplane. With help from the soldiers I moved it into the compound, not without some difficulty, but I thought it was better to put a bit of extra work in than to have an uneasy night, fearing for the safety of the machine.

We left Chahbar at 5.20 next morning. A few miles out we crossed the border into Baluchistan; the terrain all the way to Karachi was very similar to that of Persia. The first hour we made 83 miles, 2nd hour 71 miles, 3rd hour 86, 4th hour 80. Here we got well bumped about, especially when rounding a rocky promontory called Ras Malan. For a few minutes we got into a very strong head

113

wind, and, besides the bumping, the ground speed dropped to 50 m.p.h. I came down to 800 feet altitude and not only lost the contrary wind, but presently picked up a strong following wind.

Along the coast, 80 miles north-west of Karachi, many schools of porpoises could be seen in the water beneath. They looked so big I thought they were young whales, but was told they were only porpoises. Reached Karachi at 11.25 after a run of 614 miles during the morning. Here the Moth firm have a branch agency, in charge of Wing Commander Crosbie. He had been extremely surprised to hear that morning that I was on the way. Apparently no news had been heard of me since I had left Tripoli, and he imagined me to be at Cairo instead of Chahbar. He took me back to his flat, and as I needed a number of spares, and he could not collect them in less than three hours, he easily persuaded me not to carry on any further that day. He took everything in hand while I read Ludwig's "Life of Bismarck." The spares that I needed were as follows :—

2 new tyres.
1 new inner tube.
2 exhaust valves.
2 outer valve springs.
1 screw driver.
4 more plugs,

and my No. 2 petrol tank needed securing. They re-fuelled me with 40 gallons of petrol and a change of oil. De Haviland's mechanic cleaned my plugs and filters for me and adjusted my tappet clearances. At the time I was very glad to have the work taken off my hands.

114

CHAPTER X

WE left Karachi next morning at 6.45. It was a
fine moonlight morning. Flying by moonlight takes
a lot of beating, with the blue exhaust flames
burning fiercely in front as if from four huge
blow-lamps. Day broke at 7.30. I always had an
idea that India was the sort of country one got
lost in very easily, but actually the reverse is the
case. 250 miles out of Karachi we were crossing
the Thar Desert. It was most populous for a
desert, with villages and small towns everywhere.
It is true that it looked impossible to grow anything in the surrounding country, and indeed there
were no signs of any cultivation. The log book
reads :—" 1st hour 80 miles. Drift 15º, course
accurate. At 3½ hours, 270 miles—76 m.p.h.
Climbed to 4,500 feet. Excellent pineapple; many
thanks, Commander Crosbie! 4 hours, 312 miles
—42 miles last half-hour. 5½ hours, 454 miles—
94 m.p.h. for last hour and half. Nasirabad, 516
miles, 12.50."

At Nasirabad there is a cantonment. Immediately on getting out of the cockpit I felt the heat
scorching the back of my neck. I clasped my
hands to it while I discussed re-fuelling with an
officer of the cantonment who came out to offer me
help. This was Captain Shipton. I put in a
complaint about the heat, which I considered
against the rules in winter. He assured me it was
cool compared to the summer there. I made a
mental note not to spend my next summer at
Nasirabad. He then took me off and inflicted me

on his wife for lunch. It was a delightful lunch, and I would have enjoyed it even more had I not been conscious of a week's growth of whisker. I could barely keep awake, so after lunch they lent me a bunk for a few minutes' sleep. After that I felt more ready to cope with the natives who had brought out the petrol. Fortunately, also, Captain Ambrose helped me. It is an irritating job in that heat trying to show them how to set about re-fuelling.

Before leaving I laboriously climbed back into the Sidcote suit. It might be hot on the ground, but I had determined to stick to the Sidcote till it became too hot in the air. We got away at 2.50, and I at once set a compass course for Jhansi, 245 miles further on. Several large birds like vultures flew unpleasantly close, evidently bent on examining this strange fowl of the air. One came at me bang in the eye and I dodged sharply to avoid it, remembering the case of the airman who smashed his prop by running into one. As he neglected to switch off his engine immediately, the prop vibrated itself out of the aeroplane. All the same he landed safely without the motor.

Except that my motor seemed to have taken on a harsher note, the afternoon's run was delightful, in perfect weather over interesting terrain. Knowing the enormous population of India, I was surprised to find this part of the country did not seem nearly as thickly populated as the Nile Delta, or the north of Italy. We landed at Jhansi at 5.25 after a run of 761 miles. There were three British fighters there, squatting on the landing ground. It was just luck that they happened to be there; they were in the middle of manœuvres. The pilots rather pulled my leg about it, as otherwise I should have had to spend the night in the open. Not that that would have mattered so very much, but certainly I should have missed one of the most pleasant evenings I had known for a long time. I felt too tired to do my engine that night, but did not mind leaving it till morning, as I felt I had an easy day ahead of me.

There was a marvellous hot bath in a piece of canvas, arranged in the shape of a dew-pond, and after a hearty dinner I slept like a log in the camp bed of one of the absent officers. In the morning, doing the routine maintenance of my engine, I was very sorry to find that the valves in both numbers one and two cylinders were again going. It meant that they would have to be made perfect in Calcutta, as I knew one could not play pranks with engines after Calcutta.

I got away from Jhansi at dawn, seven o'clock, wishing I could stay with those pilots for a week —they were a great crowd. It was another delightful run: at first we were passing through a thin ground mist which limited visibility to 1,000 yards, yet the ground looked most attractive through it. I set a compass course for Allahabad, 199 miles further on. Flying conditions had been so ideal recently that I began to think the trip was easy money. I was soon to discover I had thought a day too soon.

Allahabad, which we reached at 9.20, is the best aerodrome I have yet come across. 1,000 yards square, it has a surface like a table top. Whether it is equally good in bad weather I do not know. Some very obliging and efficient Indians re-fuelled Elijah. There was one Indian who had been sent out by the local Magistrate to offer me any assistance I might require. I tried the motor again.

117

It was no good. Both Nos. 1 and 2 were getting pretty bad. I could only hope there would be an efficient mechanic at Calcutta to do the dirty work for me. If I did it myself I felt I should be too tired next day to continue without a rest. Yet I felt greatly averse to being delayed; I seemed to have developed a terrific urge to get home as quickly as I could.

We left at ten o'clock. From now on the country over which we passed appeared to be teeming with people. All the same, it was not depressing, as most thickly populated parts are. There were many wide rivers to impart some sense of freedom, and some hilly country. From Benares I followed the Grand Trunk Road, with a galloping wind behind me, so that we averaged 107 miles an hour for three hours. They evidently take their religion very seriously hereabouts. For instance, I saw a mosque at the very summit of a hill called Parasnath, 4,090 feet in height. Query—do the natives all climb up to worship before going to work every morning.

I enjoyed the trip very much in spite of the engine, which was by now vibrating unpleasantly. At Katrasgarh, 320 miles from Allahabad, there was an area honeycombed with railway lines and dedicated to mining and similar occupations. The last hundred miles before reaching Calcutta was rather like travelling through the suburbs of a big city. Calcutta I never saw because smoke haze like a cloud hung over it. My compass course, which was simple to check in such easy country, took me straight to Dumdum aerodrome some miles to the north-east of the city. I had been warned to be careful in landing at Dumdum, as it was under repair, but it seemed to be an excellent aerodrome. I was conscious of slipping over a solid wall of dark green jungle as we glided in to land. It gave one the feeling of settling down in the middle of a green-walled amphitheatre. We landed at 2.45 after cutting out 687 miles in 6 hours 55 minutes. I had a feeling that I was in some way cheating by getting such easy flying conditions as I had from Tripoli to here. However, for the next 4,500 miles I was to find many little things to prevent me from thinking flying always easy.

The first thing to do on landing was to find out if my engine could be done by some person other than myself. The Aero Club's ground engineer was there, but he said he could not tackle it because he must keep his own machines fit for the next morning's flying. Fortunately Mr. Raynham, manager of the Aerial Survey Company, took both me and Elijah under his wing. A very efficient mechanic named Woolland took over the engine while I was taken to the club for some lunch. After that I returned to see how Woolland was getting on; with the natives helping him, he was already working at the grinding of the valves in Nos. 1 and 2. They had become badly pitted; and because of the air blowing through the valve seatings, there was no compression in the cylinders. This had unbalanced the motor and caused the vibration. Excessive vibration will put an undue strain on moving parts, and that combined with the great heat generated may mean a broken valve stem or other breakage which will cause the engine to smash up.

They worked all afternoon and into the evening, finishing the job about 7 or 8 o'clock at night. I was very grateful for somebody else to do the

119

work for me. The fact is, I was beginning to feel pretty tired again. It is not exactly the flying which makes you so tired, but the continual conversation and negotiation with your host for the night, and with acquaintances and officials, together with the considerable amount of work which has to be done every day on the engine. Yet careful nursing of your engine is absolutely essential to give you a chance of success on such a flight. The average aeroplane engine has a complete top overhaul every 100 or 150 hours, when engaged on its ordinary duties with flights seldom exceeding two hours in duration; whereas it is necessary to run the engine for about 200 hours during the London-Sydney run, including the time spent in warming it up on the ground and in testing it thoroughly before starting a flight. Besides, this time is not composed of flights of short duration, but mainly of flights amounting sometimes to ten hours without a stop, which is far more gruelling for an engine. One must listen attentively to its note the whole time. Every night on arrival, or before leaving next morning, I used to inspect the engine, change the eight sparking plugs, remove and clean the petrol filter, drain and replace the oil, check and adjust where necessary all tappets, grease all moving parts, fill up all tanks with petrol. Then, besides your engine, you have yourself to look after. One is usually too tired to do the engine immediately on arrival. I used to try and obtain a short sleep and a meal, and then return to the aerodrome to do the engine. You must arrange that you will have enough food and drink for the next day's flight, check over your maps to see that the existing strip will take you far enough. Arrangements must be made for sleeping accommodation for the night, and also transport to get to the aerodrome at daybreak next morning. All this time you are interviewing many strangers, in itself one of the most tiring of jobs to me. Every day during the flight I used to get up at approximately 5 o'clock, and would get to bed at about 11 o'clock at night. During this time, one can truthfully say one is going hard the whole while. This amount of work would not so easily knock you up if it were not for the shortage of sleep. If you go to bed at eleven, you are probably so tired that it is impossible to sleep for an hour or two. On top of this, although you have 16 hours of work each day, sleep, etc., cannot claim what is left over of a twenty-four hour day, for owing to the travelling eastwards, the day only totals $23\frac{1}{2}$ instead of 24 hours.

I spent a very pleasant evening at Mr. Raynham's house. He is one of the few airmen in the world who have spent a really long time in the air, and I was able to get several good tips from him. One subject I enjoyed discussing with him was the question of making a forced landing in the sea with a land plane. As far as I can make out, a land plane under such circumstances immediately dives to the bottom. At any rate there seem to be few, if any, instances of their floating. If you try to make an ordinary landing, however slow you make it, it stands to reason the plane must tip and nose over when the under-carriage catches. In this case it will surely begin to dive at once. The only chance of stopping it from diving (I invite correction on this point) would be to touch tail first in a stalled condition, a feat very few experts could accomplish. Unless someone convinces me another way is better, and provided I have the

121

nerve personally, I intend trying a broadside-on landing by swishing the tail hard round at the last moment and flopping down head and tail simultaneously. With this manœuvre it would at least be unlikely to nose over until you had had time to clear the cockpit.

I slept for the night on a bed canopied with mosquito netting. It was a decided indication that the Tropics were at hand. Next morning Mr. Raynham drove me out to the aerodrome at daybreak. The remaining Siamese aviator was due to start at the same time. I say "remaining" because there were three Siamese machines which had just visited India, and this was the only one left uncrashed. However, when we arrived No. 3 had not shown up. I gave the engine a thorough revving. It seemed to be in excellent order. We got off at 6.30. It was another fine day. As we skimmed over the top of the jungle, the palms and dense foliage of dull heavy green near the aerodrome were most attractive, once one had the idea that an engine failure was in the hands of the powers that be, and not one's own. Nevertheless we quickly climbed to 4,000 feet. Now for 150 miles we flew over a vast network of rivers and canals, seas and lakes, peninsulas and islands. For all this the great mother Ganges was responsible; we were traversing the hundreds of mouths of the Ganges River. You could look in any direction and see, apparently sprouting from solid land, the sails of some junk or other boat floating down one of these waterways. $2\frac{1}{2}$ hours after leaving Dumdum we left the last of them behind as we turned the northerly corner of the Bay of Bengal and headed southwards towards Akyab.

At Chittagong, where I amused myself by

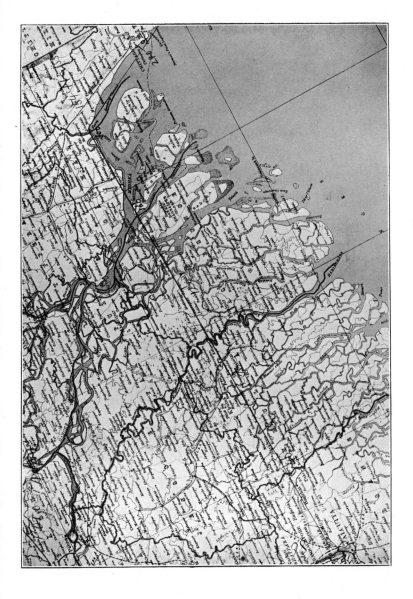

THE MOUTHS OF THE GANGES

Facing page 122

bombing a steamer in the stream with an empty
pineapple tin, I could, had I known it, have dropped
a tear much more appropriately, for here was the
milestone which marked the end of good flying
country, and now we were entering on the 4,000
miles of bad country lying between there and
Darwin. Instead of nice open country where a
forced landing could be made at a pinch, the
terrain was wild and smothered by thick vegetation, luxuriant jungle, or solid rubber plantation.
At the water's edge, where one might reasonably
expect a mud or sand bank, heavy jungle not only
grew to the brink, but even seemed to encroach
upon the water. I do not know if they were
mangrove swamps or not. Only where the open
sea beat on the shore there appeared now and then
a stretch of white beach, which looked as if it
might be suitable for a forced landing with some
safety to one's self, even if not to the aeroplane.
How many of these were thus suitable I do not
know, for it is very difficult to tell from 4,000 feet
whether a beach slopes steeply or not, and whether
the sand is soft or hard.

While slipping behind Maiskhad Island we had
to drop down rapidly to 600 feet to escape the first
storm cloud we had come across since the
Mediterranean. Its centre looked heavy, black, and
ominous, as if it contained all the furies of Ajax
pent up within it. At any rate I felt disinclined
to try conclusions.

We reached Akyab at 11.15. As I had plenty
of petrol to carry me on to Rangoon, it was not
necessary to land; but I was feeling bored and
wanted to wash my hands, so decided to come
down. The landing ground is L-shaped. With
the wind blowing from the West I had to land on

the shorter strip. As we glided down, I noticed a native walking across. He was right in the track of the aeroplane, but I did not worry, presuming that he would clear out as soon as he saw us coming for him. To my amazement he never even turned round to look. Here we were 100 yards away and he strolling unconcernedly right across our path. As I always approach and skim above the ground once before landing it would mean having to go off again and make a third circuit because a confounded native was doing something contrary to all rules and regulations. Who ever heard of anybody not ready to cast himself prone upon the ground or at least to bolt for his life when an aeroplane came straight at him? I bellowed angrily at him. Not a bit of good. In the end I was compelled to swivel to the left when just on the point of touching. This was a decidedly ticklish and rather foolhardy manœuvre to undertake, and subsequently I made a rotten landing. It is so aggravating to think that you have prevented a nigger from having his head mown off, and this at the risk of smashing your machine, while the nigger in question continues to walk on unconcernedly without even condescending to realise how narrowly he has missed a flight into another world.

One of the first men to arrive to see what had dropped in on them was a New Zealander named Price, the Port Officer of the town. He asked me if I knew Wanganui College, where he had a son. Mr. Chapman, the P.W.D. engineer, took me along to the Club for a drink and a wash. Just as we were leaving, a big Tri-motor Fokker running on the Dutch East Indies-Holland mail service arrived. It came sailing in across wind and landed without any bother at all. The cross wind did not seem to give any trouble, as it would have done me. This was the last mail plane on its way home from Batavia. The service has been stopped because the British declined to let them fly over India until the aerodromes had been improved. We formed a queue of two waiting for the petrol pump, a somewhat unusual occurrence in this part of the world.

I had landed in sheepskin thigh boots, Sidcote suit, fur gloves, and generally complete Arctic outfit. The Sidcote suit is composed of woollen lining, an exterior of rain-coat material and an intermediate layer of oilskin. An hour and five minutes later I took off again in shirt sleeves; even in them I had been thoroughly roasted while on the ground. The Dutchman took off across wind without experiencing the least perceptible difficulty. As the drift appeared to have no effect on him, I thought the wind must have dropped, and took off the same way. I thought it was good enough for me if it was good enough for him, but I made a big mistake. With my back petrol tank full it takes the plane a fair run before the tail will lift off the ground, and naturally after that it takes longer than usual to get off. Before we got up enough speed to give me sufficient aileron control to enable me to side-slip into the wind to counteract the drift, we had developed a tremendous drift, and I became frightened the under-carriage would sheer off. We left the ground with the port wing tip practically scraping it, and after that just cleared the tree-tops. I made a strong mental note that taking off across wind in an overloaded Moth is bad for the nerves.

After Akyab the country looks nice and easy, to judge by the map. In practice it is not so. Heavy

125

jungle grows right to the edge of and into the water. As soon as the chance occurred, I slipped over the Arakanyoma, a range of hills rising to 4,000 feet and dividing the Irrawaddy valley from the Indian Ocean. After these hills we again had a hundred miles of good country to Rangoon. This we crossed in an hour, with a strong following wind. I thought there might be some fun landing at Rangoon racecourse in such a wind, but fortunately it dropped just as we arrived there. I had received cabled instructions to circle the racecourse for ten minutes before landing, to enable the racehorses practising on the course to get off it. This racecourse provides a one-way landing ground with plenty of length but no width. There were several horses galloping round when I arrived. After circling for ten minutes one of them still continued; so I raced him myself for one lap, close to the ground; I think I won by a neck.

We landed at 4.10 after a day's run of 770 miles in 8¾ hours. One is only permitted to land here by courtesy of the Rangoon Turf Club, but once you can get permission they certainly give you an excellent time. Mr. Freeman, the resident engineer, put me up for the night. He had previously put up most of the pilots who had flown along this route—Berk Hinkler and the German pilot, Kingsford Smith and crew, and Moir and Owen. He showed me an interesting photograph of the German pilot, a Count, standing by while a priest blessed his machine and poured Holy Water on its nose. Mine has often been blessed too, but not in the same sense. This German was a great fellow, flying a small Klem-Daimler monoplane. The engine is of 40 h.p. with only two cylinders and one magneto. He was making a " Round the

126

World " flight with this baby machine. Of course he shipped it over the stretches of sea, but his was really a stout effort. I remember his arrival in California when I was over there. Mr. Freeman said Moir and Owen would never be able to " put on dog " with him, as they had been forced to retire to bed in his house while their shirts were washed.

In the morning we got away at 5.35, just on dawn. When leaving, I flew round an enormous wooden reclining image of Buddha. Mr. Freeman had told me that it was the biggest of its kind in the world. It formed an obstruction to be carefully avoided by aeroplanes. One had the feeling that on flying round the back of it, one was getting a glimpse behind the scenes; the straight, plain, flat-boarded back looked as if it was not meant to be seen by the public.

For forty miles east of Rangoon I witnessed a curious phenomenon. The terrain is perfectly flat and cut into tiny allotments. Everyone had lit a fire to cook his bacon and eggs, or whatever the natives here eat for breakfast. There was evidently just enough breeze to blow the smoke away from the huts as it emerged, and this produced the curious spectacle of hundreds of lines of smoke from one to five miles each in length and all pointing in the same direction. Furthermore they always remained the same size and at the same height from the ground as when they first left the hut chimneys, so that in some instances the smoke from one house joined the smoke from another house two miles to the south, the combined effect resembling a taut clothes-line strung between houses and stretching to beyond the limit of eyesight.

127

CHAPTER XI

AFTER leaving Moulmein, 120 miles from Rangoon, we began to fly over the prettiest stretch of country along the whole route. Perhaps on land the colours might seem too bright, but from the air the general effect was superb. The various shades of blue and purple among the mountains, the luxuriant vegetation of dark green and deep brown, the marvellous blues and greens of the sea, here and there short stretches of snowy white sea beach. From a flying point of view it is most unpleasant, there being no landing fields along the 610 miles of route between Rangoon and Victoria Point. There is supposed to be an emergency landing ground in a playing field at Mergui, at the 420 mile peg, but I should say, after looking at it from the air, that although one might land there, it would be impossible to move the aeroplane out of the field except in a cart.

When we got to Victoria Point I could not see any sign of an aerodrome. The thing most nearly resembling one was composed of the tailings from a tin dredge. After scouting round for a bit in vain, the bright idea dawned on me that this was an unnatural place to build an aerodrome anyway, so perhaps my map was wrong. I asked myself what would be the most likely place to build an aerodrome in this locality. The answer seemed obviously to be " near the sea," whereas I was inland from the Pakchan River, so I bowled over to the sea and found the landing ground immediately. It turned out that the place indicated on my map as Victoria Point was a Siamese town, Mt. Ranong. The Air Ministry notice of Victoria Point landing ground said it was 1,560 yards long, that it was under repair, and that care must be exercised in landing. It was a terrible spot, shut in by hills covered with palms and jungle, and with a young mountain seeming almost to hang over it on the eastern side. In my first effort to land I over-shot badly. The second time, although I seemed to be only a foot or so above the pole stuck into the ground at the corner, it looked as if I was going to over-shoot again. I thought my judgment must be very wrong to over-shoot a 1,560 yard field. I side-slipped and put old Elijah down very firmly with quite a considerable bump. Even then, we only just stopped at the far edge of the field, because of the down-hill grade at this point. On inquiry I found the field was not at this time 1,560 but between 300 and 400 yards in length; however, I was informed it would be 1,560 yards when the unpleasantly large hill in front had been levelled off and incorporated in the aerodrome. Meanwhile, that spot is a death-trap for mug pilots.

Mr. Russell, manager of the Heved Rubber Estates, came out to meet me and offered to put me up for the night at his place. He said, as perspiration flowed off him in streams, that there was nowhere for me to go on to. This was annoying, as I felt I could have added some more to the 610 miles we had done. A crowd of Malays and Indians pulled Elijah along the road to his house. The heat was intense, and I was very grateful for the chance of a cold bath, followed by a few minutes' sleep. Mr. Russell helped me do the engine after dark. He had a very pleasant house built up some twenty feet off the ground and reached by externally situated steps. Mrs. Russell warned me that I should probably be kept awake by the weird noises issuing from sundry animals in the jungle, so that I should not have been surprised to find a tiger sleeping in my cockpit next morning. However, the only denizen of the jungle which I suffered from was a small fly that crept into the pilot tube of the air-speed indicator during an unguarded moment. This must have proved more unpleasant for the fly than it was for me. Fortunately there is another variety of A.S.I. on the starboard interplane strut.

Next morning another crowd of natives pushed Elijah back along the narrow road to the field. The thing to do was to find the longest run on the aerodrome. I felt as nervous as an old woman might have been. It was absolutely imperative to have a full load to make a non-stop run to Singapore, yet the landing ground seemed altogether too small for taking off with it. I walked all over the field and finally decided against the run which was actually the longest. This was because it had straight ahead of it the palm-covered hill, and it looked as if it would be about an even chance whether one could get over that or not. There was a road winding through the jungle and I debated whether I could perhaps twist along the clearing made by the road. If I picked a slightly shorter run across the field there would be obstructions at the end of it, but slightly easier to clear. Finally I decided on the latter. Either way it was not pleasant. I remember repeating time after time to Russell, " I don't like it," but he didn't seem to mind. I was told that Moir and Owen when taking off taxied round the aerodrome to get up some speed before turning into the straight. One has to be pretty desperate to try an expedient like this. At any rate it would end in disaster if I tried it. I gave Elijah full throttle; she seemed to gather speed more slowly than a snail. In one's imagination it seemed an age before even the tail lifted from the ground to taxi. We just crawled across the field and were still sticking firmly to the ground when we reached the wire fence at the end. At the last minute I yanked the nose up and hurdled over the fence in that exceedingly unpleasant stalled condition. But that was only one step. Straight ahead, a wall of palms. Again I kept Elijah's nose down till the last minute, in an attempt to get up some speed, and at the last moment yanked her over again. Altogether Elijah only just managed it both times by the dust of her wheels, and this episode ruined the whole day's fun for me. A bad take-off and a bad landing are unreasonably annoying. There is only one way to fly properly, and that is to take no risks, so that every time you take a risk you feel that you have flown badly. I suppose it is an imitation of the feeling that an artist has when he paints or writes badly. Here is an extract from the log book at this point :—

" Left Victoria Point 6.55. First hour 76 miles (got off Victoria Point by the skin of my teeth). Revs. 1,720 to 1,730. Air speed—68 miles an hour. Height 3,600 to 4,000 feet. Have come 34 miles further by coast route. Distance—3 hours, 224 miles, equals 75 miles per hour. No. 1 tank empty at 10.45. 10.55, 314 miles. Last hour 90 miles. Good. Fix of 363 miles at 11.37 equals 70 miles per hour. Can see wind going four different directions by smoke on thousand acre flat plot. Bumpy

air. 11.55—Penang, equals 368 miles. Last hour
72 miles. Average so far, 77 miles per hour. 6
hours, 466 miles. Last hour 80 miles per hour.
7 hours, 554 miles. Last hour 88 miles per hour.
8 hours, 699 miles. Last hour 75 miles per hour."

The first part of the trip from Victoria Point
was over the same magnificent scenery as the day
before. The inlet at Victoria Point looked grand
just after dawn, with wisps of mist lying about on
the perfectly still surface of the water and on the
jungle growing to the water's edge. I flew down
the sea coast behind countless islands. The
stretches of beach here and there provided the only
possible chance in the event of trouble. We kept
on the seaward side of the tongue of land called
Ko Puket and jumped its back just south of B.
Klok Kloi. This brought us to a huge bay of
islands. I steered over the top of one small one
about 200 yards in diameter which stood several
hundred feet out of the water. The centre was
quite hollow and a tiny lake circled by a narrow
strip of beach lay at the gloomy bottom. I headed
for M. Krabi across the bay, and thence down the
coast again. The weather so far was superb. At
Perlis slight relief to the unkindly nature of the
terrain was afforded by a 100 mile long plain
intensely cultivated. Every fifty miles or so we
would pass a stretch of beach or a straight piece
of road, or a bit of paddock, where one might
possibly have got down with comparative safety in
the event of a forced landing, but taken on the
whole, it is all rotten country for flying over in a
land machine. This plain lasted to Penang, which
was an interesting-looking town. Many ships lay
off George Town in Penang Island, and the town
appeared to be teeming with life.

After Penang, we made our first acquaintance with the monsoon. At the start, a few scattered clouds; later they became black, heavy, and more frequent. By the time we were abreast of Kwala Lumpur the air was hot and steamy, and we were dodging in and around storms constantly. Every now and again, unable to avoid them all, we would catch a heavy downpour for a few minutes. I had a reserve supply of petrol waiting for me at Kwala Lumpur, but had been strongly advised not to attempt a landing there unless absolutely necessary. The landing ground was said to be dangerous. Abreast of Kwala Lumpur, on the sea coast, all the inland country being completely hidden by heavy rain and black clouds, I took careful stock of my petrol and decided I had enough to take me the remaining 205 miles to Singapore without re-fuelling. I suppose if one made this trip again, this tract of country would appear quite easy, but at the time, after seven hours or so in the air, tired, stiff and cramped, flying over bad country with the weather getting worse every mile, it was a most dreary trip. One has a strange feeling of unreality; the heavy steamy growth seems un-natural, and flying an intrusion upon a hot-bed of nature where life and growth are common and of little value. The storm clouds contributed greatly to the feeling of unnaturalness, as if one were fly-ing in a strange planet, and what was the sense of it anyway? The best thing to do is to use auto-suggestion as strongly as possible and reason with yourself that a perfectly good landing ground is waiting with ordinary appurtenances thereto and ordinary human beings about the place and there-fore there is nothing to worry about. In practice it is not as easy as it sounds in theory.

Several times when we ran into particularly heavy weather, I turned back until we were out of the storm, and then went round it, sometimes a good way out to sea. The run from Kwala Lumpur seemed interminable. Storm after storm. Even when we got to Singapore Island we still seemed to plug along for ages before the aerodrome came in sight. We landed at 4.55, after ten hours in the air for a run of 779 miles. Group Captain Cave, and the officers of the 205th Flying Boat Squadron, stationed there, took me along to the mess and plied me with a very welcome whisky and soda. I felt too tired to do the work on the machine that night, so deferred it till the morning.

After a pleasant dinner at the mess I sat for a while listening to yarns. I told of the Italian pilot who said he had crashed 17 machines, to which they replied with the story of a certain flight-commander during the war who by virtue of his rank still flew after writing-off his 35th machine. In repairing his most recent crash the mechanics fitted too short an under-carriage by mistake. As soon as the gallant Major got his tail up when taking off, the propeller wanged into the ground and over she went on to her back. By unanimous consent the Major was allowed this accident free.

The story of the crash of two airmen flying an explorer-publicist home was amusing. On reaching Athens the authorities demanded whether they had any cameras on board. " Oh no, not at all," was the reply. Off they went. Unfortunately they hit the fence at the end of the aerodrome before the plane got its tail up. Result—sticky mess. The sad part of the story is that the plane on breaking its back disgorged therefrom several hundredweight of cinema and other cameras stowed in the tail; these had kept the plane's tail down and caused the crash.

After a few more yarns I went to bed. This operation consists of lying as nature produces one, on top of a bed, complete with pillows and bolster, and the whole enshrouded in mosquito netting.

Next morning after breakfast at the mess I was driven round through a rubber plantation to the hangars at the far side of the aerodrome. The plantation was by no means thrilling. Row after row of trees with exactly the same spacing between, each with its bark scarred in herring-bone pattern and a little cup hanging from the end of one scar. They looked so orderly, so unromantic, so tame. One would think poultry-farming more romantic than wet-nursing a battalion of immobile trees. At least the cockerels scrap together sometimes.

After re-fuelling with 46 gallons of petrol and two of oil and going through my engine maintenance, I said good-bye to the pilots and took off at 7.42. The only things I didn't like were the formalities of advising the British Consul at Batavia that I should be arriving at 3.30, and all about myself. With an aeroplane it is always uncomfortable to say you will arrive at some place at a definite hour. It is asking for trouble. Also I knew how well the Dutch treat visitors and with how much ceremony, so that it would be all the more unfortunate if I could not arrive to time.

I set a course of 190 degrees and began climbing straight away. The first eighty miles was over the sea, which is here dotted with a number of small islands; but as far as I could make out, the only advantage of having them there was that one would not have so far to swim in the event of

135

going down, because there was no room to land on any of them. I climbed above the clouds, which were covering about seven-tenths of the sky. As we neared Sumatra they grew thicker and higher. We made Amphitrite Bay, Sumatra, at 9.02 o'clock, having averaged ninety miles an hour so far. Here, having the sun at the side of my neck, I pulled out the topee Mr. Russell had given me at Victoria Point, and fitted it on, but a few minutes later, in adjusting it, it blew overboard, much to my disgust. I could see it twirling down towards the sea, and wondered if some ship would collect it, thinking maybe it was something valuable. The log book here reads:—

"Height, 5,000 feet.
Revs., 1,740.
Oil, 44 lbs. sq. in.
Air speed, 68 miles."

I got another fix at the 160 mile point at 9.25. The log book reads:—" 40 miles in 23 minutes— 104 m.p.h. Cheers!"

Here I changed course to 155 degrees. From now on we began to climb steadily as the clouds increased in depth; they were sugar loaf in shape with bases absolutely flat like the bottom of cakes fresh from the oven. We had now reached a height of 7,500 feet. I felt very contented and recalled to mind the expression of "up in the clouds." It certainly was very pleasant floating among the billowy white masses in the sunshine. However, I did not want to continue climbing indefinitely, so we zig-zagged our way down and shot through into the clear space below them. The map shows at this point swampy ground underneath, exactly as the map showed for the Salt Marshes in North Africa. That was one reason

136

why I felt so pleased with things up above the clouds. I pictured the nice easy terrain underneath in case of forced landing. Sandy stretches with a little water here and there, but insufficient to prevent a comparatively safe landing. The bottom of the clouds (the floor as you might say) was about 2,000 feet above the earth. Dropping through them was exactly like entering a steam laundry in full swing. One was struck in the face by hot steamy air. When I came to look round for my nice easy forced-landing marshes they were anything but present. Instead, stretching to the horizon in every direction, was an absolutely unbroken tangle of solid jungle. Not a break to be seen anywhere. No stream or river, or clearing; not a sign of human beings. I tried to work out what I should do if I had to land in that stuff. Obviously no sun ever penetrated through the solid dark green canopy of tree-tops. Clouds of steam could be seen rising from it in different parts. It would be difficult to imagine a more solitary spot; I should think the middle of the Atlantic would seem sociable compared to it. The only thing to do in the event of coming down there would be to hack a path northwards or southwards until one expired or found a river—whichever occurred first —then go sailing down the river in the rubber boat, shooting the breakfast en route with the air pistol. Later, when I tried out the air pistol, it took me four weeks steady sniping before I potted a sparrow, so that on the whole I am dubious. . . . I do think that instead of putting every obstacle in the way of airmen carrying firearms, the authorities should insist on their taking a rook-rifle on long trips.

As far as the air was concerned, it was like

wending one's way through a gigantic forest of colossal squat mushrooms, dirty white in hue, the tops of the mushrooms being represented by the flat based clouds, and the stalks—as wide as they were high—by the rain pouring from the middle of the clouds. Here and there the sun found its way between the mushrooms, brightening the heavy green of the foliage in circular or oblong patches. While traversing these patches one glimpsed the blue sky as if seen through a chimney, of which the walls, 7,000 feet high, were composed of blowsy cloud. When under the clouds their presence weighed on one heavily, oppressing one. Filmy mists of steam drifted off the jungle, doubtless where the rain had soaked the forest just previously. Altogether it was a most undesirable location. I decided to make for the foot of the hills where the map showed a railway line. This meant civilisation, so I changed course and headed S.W.

The wind down below had turned round to west-south-west, so that my resultant track was nearly south. The wind grew so strong that I judged we were only making forty miles an hour. An endless fatiguing game of blind man's buff ensued as we zig-zagged among the rain-storms, dodging many, but every now and then getting round one only to find a wall of rain lying ahead. It stung as if it were hail, so the drops must have been exceptionally large. I thought that jungle was never coming to an end. The weather became steadily worse, and an hour and a half after striking the jungle we were dodging storms the whole time, and were steadily forced lower and lower as the cloud ceiling descended. It became harder and harder to dodge all the time. I had now to head through quite a lot of them, and it was decidedly unpleasant. The head wind against us was finally "a regular Sumatra." All the time I was searching for signs of human habitation. Presently we flew over a river, but the wall of trees only yielded grudgingly to it at its very edge. There was no trace of humanity till we had been traversing the jungle for $2\frac{1}{2}$ hours, when another river showed up. On one bank a narrow strip of perhaps a hundred yards in width had been cleared for a short distance, and here, most picturesquely, squatted a dozen native huts with dark thatch and overhanging eaves. A little farther again we came to a narrow cutting through the jungle. In the centre of it lay a snake-like pipe line writhing and twisting as far as the eye could follow it.

The sky was now completely overcast and the clouds lay heavy and sullen, closer to the ground every mile we advanced. Shortly after seeing the pipe line we struck clearings and huts, in fact genuine signs of habitation. Then suddenly we came to quite a town with a landing ground; judging from the configuration of the roads, and a railway line, I determined it was Lahat. Lahat is at the edge of the hills, and here at last the cloud met the ground, so that we had run into a cul de sac. I was forced to turn sharply and double back east to escape from the impasse. Presently we were able to rise from skimming the tops of the trees to some 200 or 300 feet above them.

The country was most unpleasant for flying. I believe the forest produces native rubber, and certainly it was now thinly populated. But for six hours, apart from the landing ground at Lahat, I saw only one spot where one could possibly have faked a forced landing. In addition to this the weather was now quite disgusting. As soon as we had cleared the foot-hills on the east of Lahat I changed course again to south-east by south and we plodded along our weary way for hour after hour. I thought we should never reach the coast. Finally, seven and a quarter hours after leaving Singapore, we hit the coast east of Talokbetong. Here the storms were heavier. There was one big black fellow straight ahead, but as it was not raining underneath I held on my course. However, it must have been waiting for us, for immediately we got under the middle of it the whole affair seemed to drop on us. It was the heaviest rain I have even known. I thought, " This is no good to Georgie," and turned promptly right about to get out of it, but before I had made half a turn we were so completely enveloped that the sea underneath was obscured from sight and, of course, there was no horizon anywhere to be seen. Nothing, in fact! It is reasonably easy to fly " blind " provided you keep on your course; but, caught like this in an almost vertical bank, I lost all sense of direction; the compass was swinging owing to the turn, and I did not know whether we were " right side up with care " or wrong side down without it. The only thing to do was to sit tight and look in as many places as possible for the sea to appear. The difficulty on an occasion like this is that you over-correct your movements. You start diving like fury and think you have corrected the fault, only to find you are now side-slipping badly or going round in a tight circle. It is very difficult to say what you *are* doing.

When the sea finally appeared we were at that moment diving straight into it. We flattened out about 100 feet above the water and, making for the coast line, tried to get through the rain that way, but the visibility was so rotten and the air so unpleasantly bumpy that I thought it was safer to turn back. After hanging about a bit on the edge of the storm, hoping it might end as abruptly as it had started, we went straight out to sea for about five miles and only thus got round it. While out there I did not think there would be much point in going back again to follow the coast for the few miles remaining of Sumatra, so set course straight for the hills visible on the western corner of Java. I must say I felt very tired at this point, for I really think flying in bad weather is as tiring as anything, and besides that I had left Singapore a bit weary in the morning. When we reached the mountain on the north-west corner of Java the terrain underneath changed entirely. Instead of the wild jungle and forest of Sumatra the ground here was cut up into thousands of little squares of water, which I took to be rice fields. Every inch was cultivated, even the slopes of the Wee-bit mountain we had jumped were cut up into allotments.

I was very glad indeed when Batavia came into sight, although at the same time it began to rain again. I flew to the centre of the town and then changed course to south-east until the aerodrome came into sight, about twelve miles away. It was a beautiful aerodrome. It is curious how one always lands on the widest part, however big it is. In this case after landing I had to taxi about half a mile over to the hangars, where the British Trade Commissioner was waiting with the Dutch authorities. Among them was Mr. Koppen, the Dutch pilot who flew the first Fokker from Amsterdam to Batavia as early as 1910; also M. Borgh of the

N.E.A. Air Force. I was astonished to find several handsome Englishmen in the group. When I got a chance later I asked Mr. Bluett, the British Trade Commissioner, about this. " Englishmen ! " he said, " they're all Dutchmen, every one of them." I couldn't get used to hearing English spoken wholesale by foreigners without it being possible to detect any accent; it seemed unnatural.

It was also strange to strike a modern airport again, complete with roomy offices, lounge, restaurant and hangars, all very solidly constructed, like Croydon on a smaller scale. This was the first of the kind I had found since leaving Europe. Of course, quite a lot of the landing fields have bare hangars on them.

We went into the lounge for a whiskey and soda and discussed the route through the Indies.

Here I made a mistake. The distance from Batavia to Atemboea is about 1,400 miles. I reckoned I could make this in two easy days' flying, but I had run out of food and needed to replenish my store. I did not think I could do a 700 mile run as well as spend an hour or two in Batavia in the morning buying food, finding out about the aerodromes ahead of me, etc. If I could not do the 700 miles there did not seem to be much point in doing any, so I said I would stop the next day in Batavia. This turned out to be a mistake, and instead of losing only one day thereby, I lost two. I do not think I would have been influenced had I known that my time from Tripoli to Java was equal at this stage to Hinkler's from Malta to Java. Anyway I didn't know and never even thought about it.

This day's run was 660 miles in 8 hours 38 minutes.

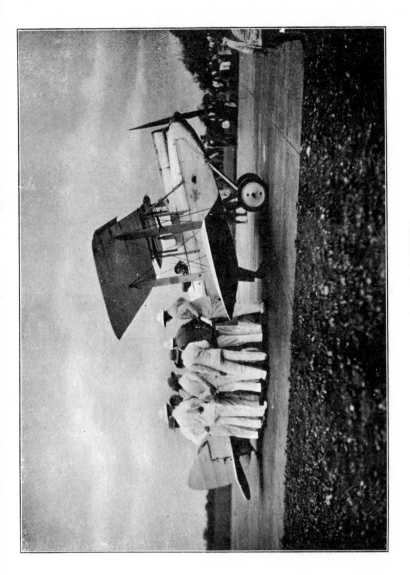

ELIJAH AT BATAVIA

Facing page 142

CHAPTER XII

I GOT more tired staying next day at Batavia than I would have had I continued flying.

I made several official calls and a number of business ones. There were many conversations with exceptionally pleasant people. Reuter's representative came along for an interview. Mr. Kraijenhoff took me off to buy stores and do my engine. In the large single-storied hotel suppressed human life seemed endlessly to rustle and whisper. In fact I could not rest, and when I left, felt a degree of nervous exhaustion I had never previously experienced. Then, too, it seems a most exotic spot. The air hangs about so moist and heavy that you feel you could hit it if you had a fan in your hand.

The town teems and swarms with humanity. Trot, trot, trot, go the ridiculously small ponies drawing higher-class Malays in a carriage which appears a cross between an ice-cream cart and a goat-cart. Thousands of modern motor cars have only the old squeeze-bulb horns which are blown incessantly.

The latest in ferro-concrete office buildings line one side of a street, while on the other side runs a muddy canal where hundreds of Malay women launder their clothes. They must be frightfully dirty to improve in the process. Thousands of pedestrians patter along barefooted, a springy bamboo pole on one shoulder, a piled-up basket of produce bouncing at each end like the balances of Father Time.

Some of the native women, especially among those in the canal, with their wet clothes clinging to their waists, hips, and breasts, were most seductive. One can understand their looking like Eve to their white masters, but I grew curious to know whether the huge half-caste population had arrived through the super-attractiveness of the women, through carelessness, or through intention. I did diffidently mention that I took an interest in this question—entirely from a scientific point of view of course—but was recommended not to pursue my investigations in Batavia.

It is an extraordinary thing that a big island like Sumatra has so very few people on it, when Java lies only twenty miles away with its forty million people. I thought at first that different administration was the only thing that could account for this, but was told on inquiry that Sumatra is also Dutch. The Javanese are great home-lovers and will not move to the other island. Yet Sumatra, they say, is a mine of potential riches. It makes you think that the world can still grow food for a tremendous increase of population. On the other hand, when you see Java cut up into little garden patches the idea is extremely depressing. I suppose the average Javanese is born, bred, lives out his life, and dies all within the area of 1,000 or so acres. What are his habits and ambitions? Yet if you look at it from another point of view, the city dweller lives on a bit of ground only a few feet square.

Kraijenhoff, of the Petrol Co., was a very pleasant companion; it was impossible to tell him from an Englishman except, perhaps, by his extra good looks and by the positively toneless and unheated manner in which he introduced into his conversation the ultra-hottest English cuss words and slang. Each time he cussed you looked up with a start expecting to see the beginning of a fight, only to find him smilingly describing some everyday triviality.

In buying a fresh store of food I was guided by past experience. I kept most of my grub in the front cockpit, having cut a hand-hole through the back to enable me to grab them en voyage. The trouble with this scheme was that petrol overflowed each time the cockpit was filled. I used to eat rather absent-mindedly, and one day at the conclusion of a packet of biscuits, bought in Tripoli, I became aware of a decidedly unpleasant taste in my mouth. On closer investigation I found that every biscuit in every packet had been saturated in petrol, not to mention the chocolate, the cheese and the dates, which latter had fermented and were almost rum (of the alcoholic variety) before I threw them overboard. So now I bought only tinned stuff—biscuits, tinned cherries, tinned pineapple, fish, meat, tinned everything I could think of. When it came to stowing them in the plane I took care not to put any big stuff near the hand-hole, for I had already been forced several times to make enlargements to it in the air with the tin-opener. For instance, while flying over India, when a large tin of pineapple got jammed in this aperture, like the cat's head in the kettle. A big tin of biscuits fitted nicely under my seat against the control-box.

Kraijenhoff very kindly undertook to ship a lot of my gear from Batavia to N.Z. This enabled me to leave behind my boots, coat and hat—all of sheepskin—besides a lot of papers and one or two novels I had read on the way out. Altogether I got rid of 21 kg. of stuff, or 46 lbs.

Next morning Kraijenhoff drove me out to the aerodrome and I left Batavia at 6.40. The maps of the Dutch East Indies are extraordinarily bad. The best one I could find for this part of the world was 64 miles to the inch, which is too small for flying. 64 miles to the inch is $\frac{1}{4,000,000}$ natural scale. I think the one millionth maps, or about 16 miles to the inch, are ideal for cross-country flying. A lot of pilots in England used to laugh at my millionth scale maps, thinking even these too small. Larger scaled ones are usual in England, but they seem unnecessarily good for cross-country work. If you use maps larger than a millionth they show too much detail and your brain gets fatigued. The point is, you must find on the ground every map-mark crossed by your track. Only when lost is it necessary to find out where land marks are to be found on a map. In a map of four miles to the inch you must watch the ground the whole time because the map is so full of detail; whereas with a millionth scale map only the prominent land marks are shown, and if you only have to look for these there is time for other things. With this method you may, if you get sleepy, over-shoot your destination by ten miles or so, but what is that in ten hours' flying compared with the extra strain of having to glue your eyes to the ground the whole time?

There are two maps much used in Java. In one of these, the distance from Batavia to Samarang is given as 324 miles, whereas it is actually 260

146

miles. Originally it took me a long time to decide
the actual distance, but after checking up on four
big atlases, including the one at the Air Ministry
in Whitehall, and using the figures of longitude as
a final check, everything seemed to point to the
correct distance being 260 miles. In the second
map used in the East Indies the distance is shown
considerably less than it is. It makes the distance
from Sourabaja to Atemboea in Timor to be 750
miles; whereas it should be about 960 or 970 miles,
according to where you cross the water-jump to
Timor. Now, this means a tremendous difference,
because 750 miles is a reasonable day's run even
in the Indies, but 960 in the monsoon time of year
becomes decidedly risky when the final aerodrome
of the day's run is 510 miles from the nearest
previous aerodrome known to be usable. Suppose
you get to Timor as your destination and find the
monsoons so heavy that you cannot get over the
hills between the coast and the aerodrome, or
suppose you cannot find the aerodrome, or suppose
that the aerodrome is under water, which means a
certain crash in that part of the world, it would
be frightfully humorous to find you were 500 miles
from the last aerodrome, especially if it were night-
time and you only had enough petrol to take you
back 450 miles of the distance in any case. An
extraordinary thing is that the Fokker pilots at
Batavia positively affirm that the distance is only
750 miles. In fact we got quite hot and bothered
about it. Later, at Sourabaja, the director of that
aerodrome also vehemently asserted that 750 miles
was the distance, so that I wondered if my map,
carefully checked up though it was, could after all
be wrong. Anyway I was not going to take that
sort of risk, so I stuck to my own map, which

showed the distance to be the greater. Finally the matter was settled by the resident officer at Bima, who, although he had had nothing to do with aviation, declared that he knew that the scale of their map was incorrect. It seems very important to be not only absolutely conversant with, but also absolutely sure of, the maps along the whole route before leaving England, and you must be exceedingly careful about accepting on the route any information differing from that on your own maps.

Information about aerodromes is also extremely confusing and worrying; for example, here is the case of Koepang, in Timor. They are building a very fine aerodrome there. In Batavia I was told by M. Borgh, the military pilot, whom the Dutch Government had asked to meet and instruct me concerning the landing grounds in the East Indies, that Koepang was not to be used. A civil pilot at the same place said it was excellent and much the best place for hopping off from for Darwin. At Sourabaja I was told it was unusable. At Bima, I was told it was in first-class order, whereas the aerodrome I was going to was unusable. By this time, growing desperate about the matter, I jumped at the Resident's offer to find out about Koepang from the Resident of Koepang himself. He settled the matter by stating it was bad in one place, making it slightly dangerous for landing, whereas Atemboea was in excellent order. All the way along the route I found the same difficulty in ascertaining the state of the next aerodrome. The best course seems to be to treat all information received as unreliable, unless the donor of it has himself landed on the aerodrome in question not more than a week previously. There is no doubt that a pilot must never act on information received unless in his own judgment he absolutely agrees with it.

The atmosphere on leaving was moist and sullen. The sky was overcast, but there was no wind.

I got a fix at the 40 mile mark at 7.7, and was just over Cheribon at the 120 mile mark at 8.53, but did not spot the landing ground there. Almost immediately after Cheribon a heavy rain-storm blocked the path ahead. I went south for ten miles, edging round the storm, but turned the corner of it only to find a bigger one ahead. This stretched right to the mountains, so I turned north again and made for the coast. Here it was extremely heavy. I came down to 150 feet and went into it. It was like flying through a heavy shower bath. I throttled down to 60 miles an hour, while a young brook found its way down my back. We came down to less than 100 feet. It was so unpleasant that I turned round and decided to return to Cheribon. We had only retraced our path for half a mile when irritation at the thought of turning back made me try again. This time we got further into the storm, descending lower and lower till only a few feet above the ground. Visibility was negligible and it was nervy work watching for trees. The nearer we came to the centre of the storm the more we got tossed about. The water stung my forehead like heavy hail and streamed into my eyes, down my chest and down my back. I cussed myself for a fool and fled. " If only I can get out of this and reach a landing ground nothing on earth will budge me from it till this monsoon is finished," I repeatedly told myself. I got out of it and headed west. Thirty seconds later I had already forgotten the trouncing I had had and my declarations of " never again." Right

149

about turn: I must have another shot. Exactly the same result as before; again I fled, again I could not bear the idea of fleeing. I began flying round in circles like a hawk over a valley while I debated what to do and hoped the rain might thin out if I waited round for a few minutes.

Just at this moment, in the middle of one of the tight circles I was making, I saw swoop out from the particularly black patch ahead no other than one of the Dutch trimotor Fokkers. He was flying a few feet above the sea, perhaps fifty yards off the coast. Well, that was the limit! If he could do it, I could. I pushed right into it. Heavens! It was more like a bath than a shower-bath. My goggles were useless through the water and steam inside them. I quickly became wet through to the waist. We were now a few feet above the sea and bumped all over the place. I had throttled down to 65 miles per hour; I was afraid to go any slower. I missed the masts of a junk or fishing boat by inches. It was no jolly good. Supposing there was some obstruction ahead of which I knew nothing. I turned half left and went out to sea. About five miles out we were able to turn the worst part of this storm. Even so I liked it no better out there. It was raining, nothing was visible except a small patch of water a few feet below, and worst of all the water was exactly the same dirty colour as the rain, and it was hard to distinguish where the atmosphere ended and the sea began.

I made for land. No sooner had we reached it than the bumps began again. We plugged on till a sudden bump stalled the 'plane, causing the slots to fly open with an audible clang. Hades! there was nothing funny about stalling 80 feet over the sea. Elijah dropped like a stone. I had put on full throttle instantaneously. I thought we were not going to pick up flying speed before we hit the pond. That floppy ineffectual feeling of the control stick with the ailerons not biting the air was like shaking a dead man's hand. I pointed Elijah more downward. We were ten feet from the water. Here the extra cushion of air near the water took effect and Elijah " bit " it. We picked up flying speed and I breathed again. But that finished it: no more fooling this time. Right about turn! I scuttled back for the first landing ground I should come across, taking off my hat to the Dutch pilot who could get through when I couldn't. Curiously enough, it seemed much easier going back than forward. There was a tall-masted junk drawn up on the beach, another one just in the water fifty yards away; I quite enjoyed flying between them.

There were lots of Malays beside the boat on the beach; half of them threw themselves sprawling on the sand and the rest bolted hell-for-leather up the beach. The laugh I got out of that cheered me enormously. Yet it was dashed annoying having to turn back.

It was not long before we reached a landing ground beside the shore, for Java is the best equipped place in the world for landing grounds. Now, was it or was it not swampy? I flew round it low. It had a tangle of very coarse grass surfacing it. It looked as if it might be a perfect quagmire. But I thought that with the matted grass and the fact that I should be prepared for it to be soft, I ought to be able to work it. I flew round again to check for possible drift. There was a little wind from the east, so I glided into it to land. Immediately we touched, the ground felt soft. I put the engine on full, determined to try and keep the tail down with the slipstream should we stick, but we left the ground. I held the throttle in readiness, but next time it felt all right, so I let Elijah finish her landing in peace.

I scrambled out at once and fished out the engine and propeller covers from my departmental store in the front cockpit. The fabric covering the propeller was eaten right through in one or two places on the boss, also at the tips. Along the inside of the blades were marks as if they had struck a cloud of stones.

Next I put on a thin mackintosh which I carried, but I was already soaked to the skin. I took off my helmet and wrung the water out of it. A canvas pocket fixed to the side of the aeroplane next to the seat in the back cockpit, which is used to hold route information and other gadgets, was half full of water. As I could not turn the aeroplane upside down to empty it, I made a hole in the bottom of the canvas with my knife to let the water out. All my papers, maps and gear were soaked. While I was doing this there appeared at the other end of the aerodrome a curious sight: a stream of humanity like a swarm of ants issuing from a wood flowed in our direction. I sat tight, and was presently the centre of a hundred or so Malays. Some wore those miniature pagodas, which seem so fashionable among the coolies; at any rate they are more like a roof than a hat, and appear to be made of thin hatch. Others, of a more economical turn of mind, just held banana leaves over their heads, and very efficient hats they made too. Some of the younger element used them for other purposes, others again didn't. I wished I had one myself; but whereas one would

152

probably be an object of much admiration in one's home town if one appeared in the banana leaf hat, I feared the sight in Java would not be so much appreciated. Some of the women looked horrible, by reason of what I took to be something they were chewing, which made them look as if their thick lips were pushed apart by a dirty red tongue suffering from elephantiasis.

Fortunately I had got Mr. Bluett and Mr. Kraijenhoff to write out for me in Malay a few sentences which I might require in the case of landing among natives. I fished these out; holding them under the top wing I hoped that I should be able to read the sentences I required before the writing became illegible by reason of the spray from the rain.

The first thing I asked was: " Saja minta satu orang djaga." " I want a watchman." I put this proposition to a round-faced, jovial looking cuss who seemed to be very contented with life. The first thing I thought when I saw him (for he stood out in the crowd) was, if ever there was a bachelor, here he was. A bachelor in Java is probably a man who has not more than four wives. He tapped his breast, beamed all over his face, and said something which included the words, " Orang djaga "; so I too tapped him on the breast and said, " You Orang djaga." He seemed to agree that he was, so I led him round the aeroplane, at various points imitating a housewife shooing off the geese. He seemed to understand this all right, so I had a shot at my next sentence, which was, " Pangil orang mata-mata." " Fletch a policeman." That is one of the advantages of flying over country where you can land, because, when in doubt, stop and ask a policeman. He seemed to understand

153

this, although I had to try the pronunciation in three or four different ways. Presently up rolled the policeman in his little skirt. He was only distinguishable from the rest by a broad ribbon hung diagonally across one shoulder. Also, he had an umbrella. I am afraid I eyed it a little jealously, for a nasty cold trickle was now finding its way below my Plimsoll line. He talked a lot; I notice that if somebody talks in a language you cannot understand you suffer from the old inferiority complex; so, on my part, I kept my end up by reciting " Hamlet's speech " in between whiles.

When I thought the policeman had sufficiently upheld his dignity in front of the mob I tried my next sentence: " Mana bisa kirim kawat," or, in other words, " How can I send a telegram? " He nodded his head vehemently, so I wrote out in block capitals on a piece of paper: " AERO-DROME SOURABAJA DELAYED TEGAL ARRIVE LATER." This I gave him with a two-and-a-half guilder note. He seemed to suggest that I should come along with him, so I fished out my attache case and we trotted off. The aerodrome was covered with a coarse kind of cutty grass. I walked round the first few puddles, but soon got tired of that and just waded through them. It was still raining hard, so when we came to the first cottage the policeman indicated we had better stop there for a bit. To this end he bundled all the inhabitants out into the rain and we went into the best parlour. The furniture consisted of a stretcher-bed of interwoven bamboo which filled half the room and was permanently fixed to the walls on three sides. There were one or two roof hats hanging on the wall. I then gave the inter-

154

national sign for " I want to sleep." To make this sign you put your hands together, place them against the temple, incline your head to one side and shut your eyes. The policeman seemed to understand this all right, but evidently decided it was not the place to indulge in such antics, so we trotted off again under the cocoanut trees and the banana plants. Presently we came to a very big house which appeared to be the official residence of the policeman. We entered a large room, the floor of which was of hard mud. From the roof in one corner hung a cage containing a pigeon; in another corner one with a sort of moth-eaten parrot, and in the other two corners more cages contained birds I had not seen before. But, joy of joys! in the pigeon corner was a big cane chair which I promptly made for, and in about thirty seconds was fast asleep.

An hour later I woke up, fished out from my attache case " The Last Days of Pompeii " and began to read. The room was now empty except for a very old, philosophical-looking cuss who was so adept at spitting that I wished I could take him to use instead of my little air pistol. Some slight commotion was being caused in the next room, which was separated from the front room by a bamboo curtain. One had an impression that there was a queue of femininity lined up there.

It seemed a shame to waste a golden opportunity to investigate the habits of these folk, so I sprang another sentence on the old buffer. This was, " Mana saja bisa dapet makanan? " meaning " Where can I get something to eat? " He trotted off and re-appeared with a plate full of debris covered in curry juice. It appeared to consist of the drum sticks from about half a dozen chickens.

He also produced a bowl of rice. I tried a bit of the meat, but I think it was seagull and not chicken. The rice was the dullest food imaginable. Once inside the mouth it stuck everywhere and was only coaxed down with difficulty.

After that I went to have a look at the weather. It was clearing up. I made a sign of going up to heaven and then collected my bag. We set off for the aeroplane again with two other policemen who had just rolled up. I took the covers off, started the engine, and gave the " Orang djaga " a guilder (worth 1/8). This, I had been told in Batavia, was considered a bag of money by the natives. He certainly seemed very pleased with it. No. 1 policeman of the umbrella arrived and I presented him formally with the change from the telegram money. Then I taxied to the other end of the aerodrome. After much gesticulation on my part, the policeman seemed to understand that I wanted to move the crowd of some four hundred natives now collected. He of the brolley shifted them in the end, but stayed there himself. I waved and flourished my arms. Finally, he also moved and I took off. Afterwards I discovered that I had not been at Tegal at all, but at Pemalang. I had landed there at 10.15, so it had taken me an hour and twenty-two minutes to cover the distance of fifty-seven miles between Cheribon and Pemalang.

I left Pemalang at 12.45 and reached Sourabaja at 3.35, landing in a shower of rain after a run of only 424 miles. Taxiing into the hangar at Sourabaja the machine got bogged and it was impossible to move it with full throttle. All hands and the cook had to turn out from the hangar and pull it in.

CHAPTER XIII

THE delay caused by the monsoon spoilt my chances
of getting from Batavia to Atemboea in two days,
because the next landing ground after Sourabaja
was Lombok, 310 miles away, and as I did not get
to Sourabaja till 3.35 it was too late to reach
Lombok that day. However, I was very philo-
sophic about it, because there is not much fun
flying over these islands late in the day when there
are so few landing grounds one can be sure of.

From Sourabaja to Atemboea is 970 miles, and
the only landing grounds over the whole distance
are:—(1) Grogok at Bali Island, which I was told
was no good and that it was not safe to land there;
(2) Lombok on Lombok Island: this landing
ground was described as good, but with nowhere to
put the plane for the night, and only Malays there;
(3) Bima, which I will describe later; (4) Reo, 130
miles farther on, where I was advised not to land;
(5) Larantoeka, 170 miles beyond Reo, which I
was told was bad and that I was not to land there
at all. Then the next is Atemboea.

The whole atmosphere of Sourabaja was different from that of Batavia. Everything seemed more
prosaic, matter-of-fact, commercial. This was the
Manchester or San Francisco of Java, the other the
London or Los Angeles. I went to a very large
ferro-concrete hotel, which might have been a new
hotel in any good American town. Even the head

157

waiter in the dining-room began to argue as to whether there was a place for me or not. Though I looked a bit wild and woolly, that did not prevent me from beginning to feel angry. Suddenly his face lit up with a smile and a smirk, and he said, " Ah, but ees it not Meester Sheshestaire, the aireman? From your photograffy I know you," which put me in a good humour till the end of the consomme, for it tickled my vanity to be recognised by a waiter in a hotel in Java. But the feeling petered out with the soup and I finished the dinner in a bored coma. Life seemed rather futile, a feeling accentuated by sullen skies and boggy aerodromes, besides many other things.

I went to bed and tried to sleep, but couldn't for a long time. When I did manage it, it was not long before I woke up again with my customary nightmare.

Next morning I got up in the dark as usual. Even then the town was a-patter and a-rustle with its half-million inhabitants. We left Sourabaja at 6.50 a.m., passing Probolinggo at 6.53 with the wind coming in from 200 degrees. So far we seemed to have been passing over a long stretch of mud speckled with towns. We made 87 miles the first hour. We flew within a few feet of the side of Argapura mountain, about 9,240 feet. We made 78 miles the second hour and reached Singaraja at 8.35. There are practically no forced landing spots here. From this point we were dodging storms all the way to Bima. These storms are rather curious, and seemed spitefully disposed towards us. You see very black storm clouds ahead of you, obviously water bound, but with no rain falling. They have flat bases as if cut off cleanly with a knife. The bases would be from two to three thousand feet above the sea. You sail along gaily and pass under a cloud. Whether the noise of the engine upsets it or not I do not know, but as soon as you approach the middle of it the whole thing almost invariably empties itself. Underneath you can see first a patch, then a rapidly widening circle which marks the spreading fall of rain. Outside the circle glassy sullen smoothness of the water surface. But inside—what a difference! The water appears to be boiling: it seethes and foams as the rain lashes it furiously. By Jove, it could sting your face too if you dashed into it at 80 m.p.h.! No wonder the propeller cover got damaged. I dodged as many as I could, but presently it struck me that the clouds were playing a mean, cunning game with me, for they seemed to wait till I was fairly caught underneath before bursting. "Well," I thought, "two can play at this game." So I began sneaking up to them at their own level. Then at the last moment, just when they imagined they had me, I would point Elijah's nose down to the water and dive like the deuce straight for the sea at 100-110 m.p.h., but without revving up the engine more than 1,750. Down would come the water just ahead of us, like a dropping barrage. Down we would dive, racing to get under it. At first it was rather sport, the water rushing up to meet us. We nearly always ended up close to the sea, and even then we were usually caught by a little of the rain before emerging to clear air the other side. It was all right once or twice, but after a while it ceased to be soothing. At the north-west of Sumbawa I went about ten miles out to sea to escape one of them. I think it is only the strangeness of these monsoons and one's ignorance of their power that

159

make one trouble about them. If one had been over the road before and knew the route and conditions . . . but then the romance would be gone.

The third hour we made 85 miles; the fourth hour 90 miles; the fifth hour 75 miles; and then ensued a nasty passage round the coast and down into Bima Bay. This is a narrow-gutted inlet stretching like a fjord about ten miles into the centre of Sumbawa Island. The aerodrome is right at the southern end of the water. There were one or two ships lying off Bima. They seemed strangely out of place; the country I had been flying over was so wild and uncivilised. There were some people standing on one corner of the landing ground, and as soon as I came into sight they lit a smoke signal to show the direction of the wind. The ground looked unpleasantly wet in places, so for once in a way I took great care over landing, only to find afterwards that it was as dry as a board. It seems to me that it is exceedingly difficult to tell the state of these East Indian aerodromes from the air.

The Dutch Resident of Bima came up to greet me. It was a very pleasant surprise, as I had thought there would be nobody but Malays there. It was 12.10 when we landed after a run of only 460 miles, and it was very peeving to find that I had to lose the rest of the day, yet I did not feel it safe to try that afternoon to make the 510 miles from Bima to Atemboea with no sure intermediate landing grounds; nor for the same reason could I do half the journey. As a matter of fact it was just as well that I had not wanted to go on in a hurry, because of the petrol agent there, who was rather a character. To start off with, he could not understand a word of English. Immediately I had

160

brought the machine to a standstill he rushed up with 30 or 40 natives and left a big forty gallon tank of petrol at the nose of the machine. The tank looked about ten years old, but painted on the side in large letters was the name of the brand of petrol; the painting had obviously been done that morning. Up sprang a stalwart photographer, the agent put his hand on the tank of petrol and was photographed some half-dozen times with the world's broadest grin on one of the world's broadest faces. After this he repeated the performance with two tins of oil, putting his foot instead of his hand on one of them. I had no objection to this at all, although I was not consulted in the matter, but when it came to opening the drum of petrol he had no tool, not even a hammer or chisel. Neither had he the faintest idea in the world of how to go about it, and it had to be done for him in the end by the Resident and myself. After we had opened it—and this was no light task, it was so rusty and the tools so inadequate—he had no pump for the petrol, no can to carry it in, and no funnel or filter. Altogether the re-fuelling took some time.

All the rain cleared away, and it turned out a lovely, hot, sunny afternoon, which was decidedly pleasant after the sweat of alternately cussing, coaxing and " confounding " the Malays over the re-fuelling.

The Malays here were of a different stamp to those of Java. They mostly carried knives in their belts and looked pretty fierce, in this respect entirely opposite to the Javanese, who appear comparatively tame and easy-going. There was one big fat fellow rather better dressed than the others who was fiddling about hopelessly during the re-fuelling fiasco. He was so irritating that I pushed the chisel into his hands and indicated that he might do some work for a change. This turned out to be a brick I had dropped, he being the vizier of the Sultan of the island. I didn't know such a dignitary existed. I may say he got even with me by stating he had had twenty warriors guarding Elijah all night. And warriors are not averse to a little payment . . . yes . . . no. Fortunately wealth was represented to him by a quarter guilder per man. No doubt he collared the lot.

The Resident took me back to the town, a considerable drive winding along the water's edge with bush, or rather jungle, an arm's length away on the other side. I saw some weird-looking crabs sidling about on the side of the road. And in one clearing, which stretched back 100 yards from the road into the jungle like a small bay of dried mud, I was amazed to see the long, fierce-looking horns, rolling eyes and upper parts of the heads of some ten oxen poking up through the mud. Nothing else visible—ten heads emerging from solid mud. The Resident noticed my interest. " Ze ox have ze mud-bath," he said.

A few hundred yards farther we came to another bay, and here some forty swine were at the same game, but I could only see the ridges of their backs above the mud. How do they breathe? And what if the small pig gets out of his depth into a big pig's stand? I consoled myself with the thought that they probably knew their own business best.

On arrival at Bima the Resident ordered a room for me at the " Pasangraham " or Government Rest House there. These Rest Houses are maintained by the Dutch Government, and they are extremely well run. You pay so much for a bed, and the man in charge buys food, which he cooks for you at a very reasonable charge. There is some sporting uncertainty as to what you will get, considering that he understands you no better than you can understand him. Sleeping is quite simple : you have a bed netted off against the mosquitoes, a hard mattress covered over with a sheet, a pillow for your bed and a long bolster, the use of which I am not quite certain about, but I imagine you drape one arm over it. Apart from your pyjamas you do not have any covering. As I had no pyjamas it was simpler for me.

After the evening meal I sat on the verandah and enjoyed myself hugely watching the house lizards (whose scientific name I have forgotten) chase the moths and flies on the wall. It really was quite sporting to see the large flying beetles settle and then to watch the lizards trying to make up their minds whether they would attack them or not. After making one or two tentative runs towards the beetle the lizard's valour would finally get the better of his discretion and he would make a grab at a beetle almost as large as himself, and probably stronger. The beetle would remain firm as a rock, while the lizard would fall with a plop to the floor, but right side up. Baby lizards, varying in size from the length of a pin to three inches, would come out and do battle with small moths and what not. On the whole I thought the lizards were a very sporting fraternity. I think we should introduce them into New Zealand to brighten up some of our duller evenings. I must write to the papers about it.

Next morning the Resident drove me out in the dark and I got away at 6.20. He had been ex-

163

tremely polite and pleasant to me, so when he asked
me to fly over his house for the edification of his
wife I gladly agreed. He explained where the
house was, several miles inland from Bima. It
was not till I had gone about five miles beyond that
I remembered about it. However, I turned back
and did my little act. How inordinately unpleasant
is turning back at any time! I simply couldn't
bear to traverse the ground a third time, so hopped
over the hills, and very unhealthy they were too,
being a succession of razor-backs with no width of
valley in between, and covered with sickly green
tropical growth. The wind was still blowing from
the southerly direction, and I could see the sky to
the north of the islands ahead of me laden with
many more black storms. To the south, however,
it looked fairly clear, so I worked it out that the
moisture must be condensing as the air passed over
the islands. I concluded we could dodge these
storms if we went round the eastern extremity of
Sumbawa until we came to the south-east corner,
and from there on stuck to the south side of the
islands. This proved to be the case. On the
whole I was rather a " mutt " not to have thought
of it before.

The next island, Komodo, is where the dragons
now in the Zoo come from. I searched the slopes
carefully for any signs of them, but was unsuccess-
ful. I should like to have one as a mascot.
Elijah and a dragon ought to do great work
between them. I was told that Sir Alan Cobham
is the only airman who has seen one from the air,
but whether or no this is the case, I cannot say.

The terrain along the south coast of Flores was
not as bad as on the previous islands : some of the

slopes looked as if you could fake a landing on them. At the east end of Ende Bay, 200 miles from Bima, there was a perfect little extinct volcano, and next door to it an ordinary cone still smouldering. I flew low over this one out of pure swank. I am sure all good aviators fly over a live volcano at one time or another; and if you photographed this one close up you would not be able to tell it was only 200 feet high instead of 15,000.

The weather was so calm and pleasant that I got quite drowsy and was extremely glad when we came to the point just past Tewerin on Alor Island, whence I had decided to begin the 44 mile water hop to Timor Island. At 11.40 I changed course to about south-east and headed across the sea. I read the bearing off the map in the air and do not remember exactly what it was. This was the first time I had deviated at all from the course planned in England, but the crossing planned on the map began 20 miles farther on, where there would have been less sea to traverse.

The water-jump itself proved quite easy money, but on arriving at Timor at 1.5 it was difficult to locate my exact point of arrival owing to the smallness of the map and the uniformity of the coast line. I came across a solitary house with a few native huts round it, and a road leading away into the hills behind. This I took to be Atapupu, but actually it was Batugadé, a house some five miles to the N.E. of Atapupu. Atemboea lies in a narrow valley separated from the sea at Atapupu by a chain of hills, so when I jumped over the hills at Batugadé there was no sign whatever of Atemboea. It is always slightly disagreeable not to find a place when you expect it. But it was such a grand day, and I was in no hurry, so the feeling quickly passed. I set off N.E. to check up that this really was the valley in question. It was right royally hot entering it from over the hills, like moving in front of a blast furnace. I followed up for 15 miles and then found a narrow gutted pass through which its stream emptied into the sea. This proved to me that I was in the right place. I concluded I must have entered north of Atemboea. I turned and sailed down again, closely scanning the terrain for any sign of a landing ground. Finally we spotted Atemboea in the distance a few miles south-west of where we had originally come into the valley.

The landing ground looked pretty rough from the air, but I noticed there was a strip along it about fifteen yards wide, looking as if it had been rolled, so guessed it must be all right, and landed after first shooting over to the township to let them know I had arrived. It was 1.5 o'clock, and the morning's run had been 510 miles. Here again after landing I found the whole aerodrome was perfectly solid, only patchy in places with long coarse grass, which, viewed from above, gave it the appearance of having a rough surface.

The officer in charge of a small contingent of soldiers stationed there came out to meet me. He had taken charge of the petrol which had been sent on my account. He drove me back to the township and put me up at the Pasangrahan. We had some lunch together and then he left me to snooze till four o'clock. They had to call me up three times before I finally stumbled off the bed, half-intoxicated with sleep, and got into the Lieutenant's car to go out to the aerodrome. Elijah had not been running quite as smoothly as usual on the last two days, and as I had the Darwin water ahead I set about making a more complete inspection than customary. I found one or two of the bolts fastening down the intake manifold were slightly loose, then I found a big crack in the outer casing of the manifold, so started to take the whole thing off. This is the dirtiest job possible, because the nuts fastening the manifold to the cylinder heads are so inaccessible. The officer very kindly lent me some petrol lamps to see by. Thousands of midgets, flying ants and bugs swarmed round as I worked. It was not so bad when they strolled into your eyes, but they would insist on going well into your ears, whence it was a difficult and unpleasant business dislodging them.

When I finally got off the intake manifold I found the crack did not run right through, so re-assembled it, fastening the last nut five hours after I had started on the task. At least I now felt perfect confidence in the old " bus."

After that I trotted out the rubber boat, blew it up to see that it had no leaks, took off the front cockpit streamlining, and arranged the boat in position so that I only had to pull a rope fastened round its middle and yank it out of its place in order to float it on the water. I fastened the sail, mast and oars up together with an inner tube, so that they, too, would float until I had retrieved them, provided I could get them out before Elijah sank. The drink and iron rations I had put in a sack and placed in the cockpit. I am afraid they would not stand much chance of getting out in the event of landing in the water, but still one never knows one's luck. After I had finished everything I felt absolutely confident for the morrow's trip.

I got to bed about midnight and slept very well, except for my usual nightmare about two o'clock.

I dreamt I was flying when suddenly my vision went completely, and I just had to sit tight until the " bus " crashed into something. I woke up to find myself groping along the sides of the wall. No doubt the lizards had a good scare.

I was just a trifle nervous about taking off. Although the landing ground is labelled 700 yards long, it did not look more than 400 yards. Also in that intense heat there is very little lift in the air.

I had had a short night, so slept in later than usual. I made another thorough inspection of the kite, and it was 7.30 before I took off. There was certainly not too much length to the ground. We cleared the fence by about five feet, and even then there were some tallish trees just past the fence which needed careful negotiating. However, all went well, and we headed due south across the uplands, to the other side of the island. Reaching the south coast, it was rather difficult to locate our exact position, owing to there being no distinctive feature along the coast line. Also, places marked in big print on the map, which you would think were towns of at least 30,000 inhabitants, were actually only villages of two or three houses.

We were now travelling over Portuguese territory. We followed the coast line for about 70 miles until we reached the point of land where I had decided to begin the water crossing. Elijah was running beautifully, and everything seemed to be in perfect order. As a perfunctory duty, I set about checking the petrol pump on both tanks. My equanimity was completely shattered when it sucked futilely, and without result. I thought perhaps the washer was not gripping properly, although this had not occurred before. I pumped away furiously for about two minutes on the forward tank. Nothing happened. I was unreasonably upset. I switched off No. 1 tank and tried No. 2—same result. That is to say, no result. I pumped away furiously for something over a minute, when, suddenly, she picked up and gripped the petrol. I switched off that tank and tried No. 1. It too worked. I was intensely relieved; it did not seem right that anything should fail on such a perfect day.

We left land at 8.20, and were out of sight of it in twelve minutes. You certainly get a kick out of crossing a good stretch of sea with a single-engined land machine. I felt moderately excited, and slightly elated. The fact is, if you are confident you have done everything possible to have your engine and plane in good order; if you have taken every precaution possible in the event of your falling into the pond, it then does you no good to worry, and it becomes a great gamble which you can sit and enjoy.

In flying over bad terrain like the East India Islands, you really have to worry; for unless you do so you will not keep searching for the best spots for forced landings, nor keep on working out what you will do in the event of having to land on this or that type of terrain. All the same, the question of coming down in the sea with a land plane is an interesting one, and I have discussed it with several experienced pilots, without being able to come to a definite conclusion about it. The general consensus of opinion seems to be that every land plane, falling into the pond, puts its nose right into it and goes straight to the bottom. Theoretically, the wings are supposed to keep the bus afloat for a short time, but I understand that in practice

169

they rarely do. It is wonderful what you are ready to do in emergencies. That is to say, theoretically, before the event. What happens in practice, it is generally fortunate nobody is there to see. Pilots often laugh at the idea of carrying a boat in the front cockpit. They say one would never get it out. I reply : If you could not get the boat out, it is probable you would not be able to get yourself out, in which case it would not matter. On the other hand, supposing you had plenty of time to get yourself out, you would feel very foolish if you had not a boat to put yourself in. And another great point about it is, to my way of thinking, that as long as you have some sort of second chance, even though it be slight, you can better put up with the idea of your main chance failing you. The same with a parachute, though I cannot speak from experience in this case, not yet having been able to afford one, but here again you have a second chance, in the event of your main chance—the aeroplane—failing you in mid-air. It is true that in most cases, when a parachute is really necessary, you do not have the time to open it; but, on the other hand, you fly easier in your mind having the idea that you have got this chance in the event of collision, etc. Supposing one got thrown out of a plane by a particularly bad bump, imagine what a ghastly experience one would go through during the 18 or 19 seconds it would take to fall, say, five thousand feet, if one had not got a parachute. I can remember filling three pages with thoughts which occurred to me in a crisis, which I have since estimated by calculation to have occupied only 3/5ths of a second.

I have been frequently asked about the trip across the water to Darwin. I must confess I rather enjoyed it because of the excitement. Certainly you ask yourself questions:—"Shall we do it?" "Why shouldn't we do it?" "Why should we do it?"

Wishing to avoid as much sea as possible, I aimed at Rocky Point, in about the middle of Bathurst Island. This would give a crossing of only 320 miles from land to land. According to one of my maps, to strike Rocky Point, the compass course was 118 degrees; according to the other, it was 120 degrees, so I split the difference and steered a course of 119 degrees. This allows for an error of nine degrees on the north side, and five degrees on the south side before one would miss Melville and Bathurst Islands altogether. Even if one missed both these islands, it would be annoying, but not dangerous, because, owing to the broken coast line of this part of Australia, it should be reasonably easy to pick up one's bearings in any but particularly bad weather. I think, on sea crossings, it is better not to correct your drift at all, unless it is very pronounced, but to note it carefully all the time, and decide where you think you are going to hit land.

For the first 100 miles after leaving Timor, the wind was coming in from north-east. At first we were drifting some 20 degrees to starboard. This gradually fell away to nothing, and for the next 100 miles there was no drift at all, and then the wind began to come in from the south-west, gradually increasing in strength till we were drifting some 25 degrees to port. I was very lucky, the weather was perfect.

The first thing I did after leaving land was to polish off a tin of kippers.

Apart from the sport, a crossing like this is apt

171

to become boring unless the weather is bad. I think it is a great pity that the octopus and other inhabitants of the deep do not come to the surface as the aeroplane passes over, it would make the trip so much more interesting. One must think only of the past, because, when in the air, it is tempting Providence to think what you are going to do in the future. After a bit, it becomes almost automatic, reading the instruments, speed-indicator, oil-gauge, level, altimeter, rev-counter, compass; you sweep your eyes over them every few minutes. As far as the controls are concerned, I see in my log book that I did not touch the joy-stick till seven bells, that is 11.30. With the tail-trimming gear, and pumping a little petrol out of the back tank, it is possible to keep perfect fore and aft trim, and with that machine it is easy to negotiate bumps by just using the rudder. In fact, I had by now grown accustomed to driving through even bad weather by using the rudder only. Fiddling about with the control-stick correcting every small bump for eight or nine hours is, I think, the chief cause of fatigue, resulting in bad landings at the finish.

My log reads as follows :—

"Left land 8.20. Tin of kippers.

2 bells—All's well.

3 bells—All's well.

4 bells—All's well. Hazy.

5 bells—All's well. Pineapple, I think.

6 bells—All's well. Pineapple lasted twenty-five minutes.

7 bells—All's well. Have flown hands off till now. Tea-oh!

11.50—Land-ho I think. If so, twenty minutes before expected. It may be a storm.

11.51—Land, O.K.—can see cliffs.

172

SOLO TO SYDNEY

12.0—' Why, here we are on land again ' (said
Barnaby Bill the sailor !)."

Visibility of Bathurst Island was not good, it
looked as if I had struck Rocky Point right in the
eye, but I turned to starboard and ran along the
coast for a mile or two, to check my bearings. It
was Rocky Point all right, so I kept on my course.
The drift, which was increasing quickly, took me
over to Apsley Strait, which I followed to Cape
Gambier. We passed over a cluster of buildings
at the south-east corner of Bathurst Island. I
could see the folks come out to have a look at the
plane, which I expect is not a common sight up
there. The country was excellent for flying, with
wide beaches, and occasional clearings in the
sparsely wooded country, where one could put a
plane down if necessary, but it looked rather dull
and monotonous. The same heavy green everywhere; it is hard to imagine a shortage of rain
here.

The rest of the trip to Darwin was easy money.
I flew over the town to let the people know I had
arrived, then flew back to the aerodrome. I could
see one or two cars tearing along the road to the
aerodrome. We landed at 1.20 after a day's run
of 512 miles. There were a few chaps there, but
when I taxied up to them, they looked at me rather
as one would look at a new species of pig for sale
in the market place. When the petrol man arrived,
he took charge of things. I remember he introduced me to a tall elderly man standing by. I
went to shake hands with him, but he said:

" No, Captain Chichester, my principles will not
let me shake hands with you until you have been
passed by the Medical Authorities."

As soon as possible I moved an adjournment to

the nearest hotel to try the local brew of beer. This motion, I may say, was unanimously carried. It felt like home to me, landing in Australia. At first everybody called me " Captain " Chichester. I explained at some length, whenever I had the chance, that I had never been in the Army, but that if they were going to promote me, why not make me a General straight off the mark? But Generals do not seem very popular, so gradually I got demoted instead of promoted.

Darwin ought to have been annoyed with me, for somebody had wired to say I would be arriving the previous day, and the whole town had rolled out in vain to see how bad a landing I should make. This mistake was due to the lack of tele- graphic communication with any of the islands after Java.

Owing to the same mistake I found numbers of congratulatory telegrams which had been sent before I arrived. I felt grateful to have avoided the disaster such an ill-omen invited.

CHAPTER XIV

I DID not have a good night's rest. I was just getting to sleep when the Health Officer arrived with a paper for me to fill in, in which I had to give a full description of my crew and cargo, the tonnage of my craft, and what ports the crew had drunk water at on the way out. I had also to give a complete list of all the ports we had called at on our way out, to state what diseases my crew had suffered from, and a lot more such questions were asked, some of which I thought were rather involved. I was rather apprehensive that he might order me to pipe all hands on deck to take an oath of allegiance to the country. However, it all came to an end after a time.

Next morning, after a shower and some bacon and eggs, we drove out to the landing ground in the dark. I gave the petrol agent the topee which the British Trade Commissioner in Batavia had given me, and I told him to offer it to the next poor devil who passed through that way, flying in the opposite direction.

We took off at 6.45. Immediately I circled round and picked up the railway, which forms a well-defined landmark for 300 miles odd, with the bush felled for a width of over a chain on either side.

The nature of the country is exactly the same for 400 miles. It is very monotonous to look at,

175

all in bush, but this is so sparse in nature that it would be almost possible to land a machine without much damage; it is not like the impenetrable forest we call bush in New Zealand. I mean that if you were up in a balloon you could easily count the number of trees beneath you.

I had two maps, the one I had when I left London, cut from a schoolroom map of Australia, and a strip map, eight miles to the inch, covering the route from Darwin to Cunnamulla, which the Civil Aviation Department had sent up to Darwin for me. However, I could see it was not going to be too easy to cross Australia with these maps. They marked places in a grand manner, so that you expected to find a town of at least 5,000 people; and when you arrived and found only three small huts you wondered if you had come to the wrong place. As for rivers: judging by the maps, there are any amount of them, but when it comes to finding them in real life, it is a very different affair. Of course, from the ground, a dry river bed must be as easy to recognise as one full of water. From the air it is very difficult to pick out a dry river bed from the surrounding country.

The log book here reads as follows :—
" Darwin—6.45.
　Brocks Creek—7.52.
　Burrundie—8.7.
　Playford—8.20.
　Katherine—8.55.
　Speed so far, 87.6 miles per hour.
　Warlock Ponds—9.35.
　No. 4 Well—10.12.
　Average so far for 300 miles, 86 miles per
　　hour.

176

Average speed for the 110 miles from Katherine to Daly Waters, 82.5 miles per hour.

Daly Waters—10.50.

Aulds Ponds—11.0. Air unsmooth."

Visibility had not been good all the way, owing to a dust haze hanging in the air, but from Aulds Ponds the visibility further decreased, and we were forced to drop within a few hundred feet of the ground. Also, the air became rough, presumably because the sun was nearly straight overhead, causing strong eddies of air to form above the heated earth. I had flown hands off so far, but henceforth had to use the control stick.

At Katherine there is the first landing ground after leaving Darwin, but the stretch between Katherine and Newcastle Waters is well equipped, there being six. They all looked in excellent condition. We passed Milner's Lagoon at 11.13, Frew's Ironstone Ponds at 11.57. Newcastle Waters is about 425 miles from Darwin. From Daly Waters, where the railway peters out, to Newcastle Waters we had been following the telegraph line, which is easy to follow through the bush, because there is a track of a chain or two in width cut for it. But in the open ground, you have to keep your eyes skinned to catch sight of the telegraph sticks.

At Newcastle Waters it was very hot, very bumpy, and a thick haze made visibility bad. Here it is necessary to leave the telegraph line and follow a track across the plain. At first I could not pick up the track, and circled round once or twice looking for it. I was tempted to land at Newcastle Waters to have a spell, but when I thought of how roasting it must be down below, when it was so hot up above, I turned down the idea, and continued the search for the track. What made it so hard to find was that there were tracks leading in every direction. I picked on the one that looked most suitable, and followed it along the rim of a great expanse of flat country, which had nothing growing on it, and appeared from the air to resemble a vast dried-up lake. The track consisted of the two wheel marks of vehicles. Mostly such a track is simple enough to follow, but gives trouble at important water holes, where faint tracks lead in every direction and your own particular track may wander off at right angles to the way it should go for perhaps half a mile or so before it resumes its correct course.

We were passing water bores about every twenty miles. These consist of a tall iron windmill, which pumps water from the bore into square ponds on either side. The ponds, I should say, are perhaps twenty yards each way.

For about fifty miles east of Newcastle Waters we occasionally met a drover or a shepherd. I was flying so low that when passing we saluted each other as if we had each been on horseback. From Newcastle Waters onwards, we only averaged 58½ miles an hour. We were thrown about in the air and it was so hot that each time I put my face out of the exhaust side of the machine I got scorched. I even wondered if the top wing, which gets blackened by the exhaust in ordinary weather, might not catch on fire in the great heat. As we were flying close to the ground where you could land almost anywhere, I did not worry much about it.

We passed the spot where Eva Downs should be,

but there was no sign of it. I believe it has been burned down. When we were due to arrive at Anthony Lagoon, according to my calculations, we came to a bore which had a fairly large tin shed attached to it. Anthony Lagoon is shown on the map as having a store, so I thought this tin shed was the store and that I had arrived at Anthony Lagoon. There were tracks leading in the right direction from the bore, but in every other direction too. I followed the most likely track for a mile or two, and then decided it was not good enough. As I had failed to pick up the landing ground near the bore I made up my mind to return and not leave until I had found it. I must have wasted twenty minutes circling round in the thick haze, about 100 feet or so above the ground, looking for it. In the end, I came to the conclusion I must have made a mistake, and that this could not be Anthony Lagoon, so we continued in the same direction that we had been following previously. A few minutes later we arrived at the real Anthony Lagoon, which, had I only known, there was no possibility of mistaking. Quite a few buildings were here, situated on the edge of a permanent lagoon. I circled and made for Brunette Downs. Once or twice I lost the track and wasted a lot of time circling round looking for it. Eventually Brunette Downs came in sight. The Manager had telegraphed me at Darwin to say that, owing to heavy rain, landing was not to be made on the aerodrome, but on the gravel patch to the north of the homestead. We had now been flying for $8\frac{3}{4}$ hours, and had come 640 miles, the last 240 of which had been most unpleasant. To land on the gravel behind the house meant a cross-wind landing, and this I did not feel up to. I selected what

179

looked like a hard patch to land on into the wind. I was flying very badly. The first time we approached we overshot. Probably it was not as big as I thought. The next shot we bumped badly. The heat makes you very irritable: I put on the engine and went off feeling decidedly peeved. We crossed over to the aerodrome, which looked perfectly good to me. We flew over it low the first time. I considered it was all right and quite dry enough, and then made an easy landing. I drank all the water I had left and lay on the ground under the shade of one wing.

After about twenty minutes a chap came walking slowly towards the aeroplane. I thought he had an enormous black beard which I could see from a distance, but on closer view I was disappointed to find it was only a youth with a fly-proof net round his face. About a million flies kept him company. They immediately attached themselves to me. I could not help thinking that as he had brought the flies he might have brought a bit of netting too. I asked about forty questions, but to practically all of them the answer was: " I don't know."

I became unreasonably irritable. I suppose there is no reason why one should expect a man living out there to know such things as who is his next neighbour. However, I did find out:—

1. That there was petrol there, as far as he knew.

2. That it was locked up.

3. That there was nobody else at the place, and

4. That the Manager was expected back some time.

My top tank was practically full of petrol. Camooweal was 210 miles away. I ought to have ample petrol to get there. I opened a tin of pineapple, drank the juice, and ate most of the fruit, giving the balance to a couple of blacks who had arrived to see the fun. I emptied three quarts of oil into the sump, and took off again, muttering imprecations upon everything and everybody. I continued to follow the track by which we had arrived. It was not going in the right direction, but I thought it would swing round later. After a while, when it failed to do so, I struck south. After travelling five or six miles south without seeing the track I decided we had overshot it, and headed north-east again. This time we picked it up after a few minutes. The only amusement I had had for some hours was reading the descriptions of the landing grounds in that part of the world. For instance, of Newcastle Waters landing ground it says :—" Petrol and oil can be obtained at Anthony Lagoon, 178 miles away. Nearest town Camoweal, 375 miles."

Of Brunette Downs the description reads :— " Nearest railway station Dejarra, Queensland, 320 miles. Nearest town Camoweal, 210 miles."

We passed over Alexandra station at 5.5. This cattle-run by the way is 12,000 square miles in extent. Most of the country here consisted of flat plains stretching to the horizon in every direction. As they had just had rain (the first for several years I understand), the mud-coloured ground had a faint greenish tinge where grass was beginning to grow; the same colour that an oat-sown field wears as the young shoots first begin to show above the ground.

We ran south-east and picked up a bore, with stock-yards as shown on the map, eighteen miles from Alexandra station. Tracks lead from this bore in various directions, and I had to circle round and round to make sure I had picked up the right one to leave by. This was irritating, because it meant burning petrol in a way I had not reckoned on.

Before leaving Brunette Downs I had calculated there were three and a half hours' flying left with the petrol which remained in the tank. At seventy miles an hour Mr. Euclid would tell us this would take the plane 245 miles, and we had only 200 to go. I thought my intention to land at Alexandra station on Avon Downs station was quite safe if at either of those places I determined there was not ample petrol remaining to carry me on to Camooweal. It had taken fifty minutes to make the distance between Brunette Downs and Alexandra station—about 60 miles—in which case we were making 72 miles an hour ground speed. At Alexandra station, therefore, I determined that the chances were favourable to my reaching Camooweal.

After the water bore eighteen miles south-east of Alexandra station the terrain began to change, the downs alternating with stretches of red soil where a few trees were growing, but so sparsely that you felt you could get away with a forced landing without completely wrecking the machine. On the other hand in these woodlands there are not many spots where you can be sure of bringing off a really good landing.

Presently, after what seemed too short a space of time, we came to another water hole with an engine shed attached; according to the map, the road from here should be straight ahead in a south-easterly direction. I circled round the bore several times, but the only sign of a road that I could see was one going due east. I followed it, expecting that it would turn south-east again in a mile or so. After following this track for six or seven miles without its showing any sign of deviating from its course I concluded I must be on the wrong track and changed course to due south, judging that the track had disappeared near the bore, but that it would reappear a mile or two further on, and that I should pick it up if I travelled south for some distance. The only trouble was that this messing round was using up my petrol supply. I was beginning to appreciate how foolish I had been in leaving Brunette Downs without a full load.

We went south for ten miles without crossing so much as a sheep track. I find that when looking for a landmark after losing your way the minutes seem to be an age, especially when you know you are travelling athwart the course you should be following. Well, now I was in a fix! I had well and truly lost the track. Under ordinary circumstances this would not have been very upsetting. With enough petrol I would have retraced our path back to the water hole and started afresh, but I hadn't enough petrol. I could not afford to play safe. I changed course and flew east again. I thought the track I had first followed from the bore must have been the right one, in which case it would turn south-east sooner or later and I should strike it by following my course east. After travelling ten or twelve miles in this fashion and not coming across any track at all, I concluded after many anxious glances at the petrol gauge that I had not enough petrol left to search a minute longer, and that drastic action was necessary, so headed in a direction which I estimated would take me direct to Camooweal. We were now flying

183

close to the ground, forced down by the visibility, which was getting worse owing to the dust haze hanging in the air. The wind had freshened up and was blowing strongly from the south-south-east. We were drifting between 20° and 25° to port and getting well bumped about. We passed various creek beds, some with water, but it was quite impossible to tell whether they ought to be on the map, or whether they ought not to be on the map, whether they were on the map or whether they were not on the map. Any of them, for all I knew, might have been the creek on which Camooweal is placed.

I had seen no traces of man's work since the water bore. A more unpleasant flight I had seldom had; I had the " wind up " well and truly. Between watching the petrol gauge, which now showed practically empty, flying the machine which was being thoroughly tossed about, and watching for any signs of a track—a difficult enough job when flying close to the ground—I did not have much time left for working out precisely or rationally the predicament we appeared to be in. By now I did not care a damn about reaching Camooweal; I was only too keen to plop down at the very first sign of human beings that we might come across, but this decision I had made too late, nothing now turned up.

We had come about forty miles since leaving the water bore. Anxiously watching my petrol, I decided I must land after another thirty miles, no matter where I might be, unless something turned up before then. That is provided the confounded stuff would hold out long enough. Approaching nightfall was now cooling off the air, but I myself felt so heated and prickly that I whipped my scarf

184

from off my neck to let a current of air blow down my back.

We were flying over flat land interspersed here and there with patches of trees. The surface of the plain was not so good as it might have been, as it appeared to be strewn with fair-sized rocks. It was becoming darker, but I carried on, desperately hoping something might yet turn up: landing in the open plain would be decidedly unpleasant. Suddenly we streaked across a scar on the ground. I banked steeply and turned back to it. At 100 feet you do not get much time to study anything underneath. At last we had struck some trace of man's presence, the first of any kind since leaving the engine bore about 55 miles back. It appeared to be a formed road running due north and south, and looked as if it might even be metalled into the bargain. It looked fine to me, but I was puzzled about it all the same. If it were what it seemed to be, why had I not known about it, and why was it running north and south? Anyhow, I flew right down on top of it to have a good look. On closer inspection the curious thing was that it appeared to be unused. However, it was to me as a straw to a drowning man, so I followed it due south, and after half a mile, or perhaps three-quarters, came to a water bore with an engine shed and a sort of hut. It looked as if with any luck there might be a boundary rider living there. I felt great relief. After the bare open plain it was like a crowded suburb to me. I must land to give myself a chance to think things over quietly. With a slow-acting brain you need time in such a situation to sort out all the facts which are presented, and to reason out clearly and rationally what has occurred.

Now, what was the terrain like for landing on?

185

Was that patch of green beside the water hole swampy? The ground elsewhere was covered with big stones and small boulders. What about concealed tree-stumps? Then there were trees dotted about all over the place just to make things a bit more awkward. I wanted to land as quickly as I could to save the petrol supply. On the other hand it was imperative to make as safe a landing as was humanly possible. There was one fair piece of ground running east and west, but the wind was blowing 25 or 30 miles an hour north and south. A cross-wind landing in such circumstances was foolish, so I was regretfully compelled to turn down this piece and look elsewhere. There was a patch of red soil to the north of the water hole which looked pretty good, only it had a tree or two on every side, and when I glided in I feared the trees ahead; they might be very awkward if I made a bad landing and wanted to leave again in a hurry after touching. I had now been eleven hours in the air, and after eleven hours one could expect to make a pretty rough landing. I pulled myself together. I absolutely had to make a good landing. To do otherwise might be fatal. I decided to try the green patch at the water hole. I flew down to within a couple of feet of it and had a good look. It seemed quite firm, but there was only about fifty yards free of big boulders. However, that ought to be all right with the strong wind blowing. I went round again and plonked one of the best landings I think I ever made. We were still running a bit when we got into the thick boulders, but I was lucky in managing to dodge them.

CHAPTER XV

WELL, I was down safely; what now? I imme-diately turned off the petrol-cock for fear I might lose a drop of what remained. I struggled out of the cockpit and dragged my legs rather than walked towards the shed which in the twilight seemed quite close; a bleaker, more solitary spot it would be difficult to imagine. There was an open shed built over the pumping engine, and the wind sighed mournfully through it. Another detached shed about six foot square stood over a large fire-place. This one was made from the sides of petrol tins, which creaked and clanked dismally in the wind. There were two or three empty benzine tins with handles, evidently used for holding water. I felt the ashes in the fireplace and fancied they had some heat in them, such as might have been left after a big fire two or three days previously, and my heart bounded with the thought of it till I realised it might be the heat of the day which had warmed them up. A benzine tin half-full of fat hung to the side of the fire shed. In a grim fashion I was pleased to find this: at least it removed starvation from the near future. I deferred further inspection of the sheds. The flies were terrible; I have never seen so many before. They crawled ceaselessly over my eyeballs, filled up my ears, and each time I forgot and opened my

187

mouth (which I did frequently, for my tongue felt swollen and stuck unpleasantly to the roof of my mouth) in flew about twenty.

The next thing I did was to have a look at the water. It was more like mud. At the edge I stirred the soft mud bottom with a stick, but it made no noticeable difference to the colour of the water. I was parched with thirst, but dared not drink any till I had boiled it.

I then went to look at the wonderful road I had come across, hoping all the time that I was on some important highway where automobiles would pass frequently. To my disappointment I could not at first even find it. Then finally I discovered a beginning of it where it sprang out of the plain from nothing. This was very queer, and after walking along it for a hundred yards or so without coming across signs of any traffic whatever, my brain began to feel congested, so I abruptly swept it clear of the whole mystery, and turning back, decided to defer inspecting any more of the locality until next day. I went over to the cockpit for a piece of paper, collected some small chips and started a fire going, the effort making my knees tremble. I took a short rest before I fetched some more chips and a couple of logs. Then I dipped a half-gallon of water out of the pool into a tin and hung it over the fire. Of all this I made very heavy weather. I do not know whether I was more exhausted than scared or more scared than exhausted.

It was now practically dark. I went out to collect the aeroplane, which I could not leave in the open because I had seen cattle in the distance; also the wind was pretty strong. I lifted up the tail and made to approach the shed, but I had not

the strength to move it that way, so I fished out a
bit of rope, and fastening it to the tail skid, proceeded to pull the plane towards the shed with a
series of jerks. Every two or three pulls I had to
rest. It took me about half an hour to shift the
machine a distance I would have managed in thirty
seconds under ordinary circumstances. Had I
started the motor, I could have taxied in in a few
seconds, but I felt that I would sooner have dug
a hole for it than have used any petrol. I hate to
think of how many flies I swallowed during the
first part of the process. Mercifully, night fell and
then they vanished.

By the time I had got the bus to the shed I felt
done. As I moved towards the fire the roaring in
my ears ceased and a black film seemed to cover
my eyes till the fire faded away and dwindled to a
pin point in the distance. I dropped on the ground
where I stood and had a rest. I was panic-
struck so abjectly that I was disgusted with
myself. I was lost, true. In not the best
country, true. I had no petrol (the only thing
that really mattered), true. But compared with
what might have been I was well off. So I
reasoned with myself, but it was no use. I was
so ashamed of my panic that I had finally to take
myself firmly in hand and determine absolutely not
to think about the matter any more until I had had
a sleep. I fetched wood for the fire, but even so
I took several rests on the way. The next thing
I did was to fish out my litre bottle of Chianti
which I had brought from Tripoli. I broached it,
not without misgiving. Yet if Minerva had let me
in for this fix, I felt I was entitled to drink the
wine. I drank several draughts, but it tasted
beastly in my mouth. I then dragged the old

rubber boat out and began to pump it up, having only enough energy to pump it half-full. I upended it and flopped on to the bottom, falling asleep in about thirty seconds. I do not think it was long before I woke again. I went over to the fire; half the water had boiled away. I took it off and stood it in the corner, tilting it on to one edge in hopes that the mud would settle, then trailed over to the water with another can and half-filled that. It was only fifteen or twenty yards back to the fire, but I was taking spells all the way. After putting this lot on to boil I turned my attention to the other. The mud did not seem to have settled much, but I couldn't help that. I dipped in the top of my thermos and drank as it became cool enough. Heavens! I've never tasted a drink its match! I finished the lot save for a slight residue of mud and slime at the bottom. I do not think I could have eaten anything if I had been offered ten pounds.

I went back to the boat and finished pumping it up. It made a wonderfully comfortable bed. Every now and then I could hear a slight rustle among the wood chips beside me, so, making an effort, I went and rescued the torch to see if there was a snake.

I soon dozed off again, but not for long, and on awakening went over to the water. It was boiling, so I yanked it off, and waiting till it had cooled sufficiently, drank nearly two quarts of it. Every few hours during the night I woke up and went over for another swig. In spite of this I was as thirsty in the morning. Except for thirst I slept passably well; I think it was about 6.0 or 6.30 when dawn came. I lay indolently on my back watching the sky, or perhaps it would be more exact to say the dust in the sky, changing colour from dark to light grey.

I began to run over all the data, and racked my brain for more evidence. There was only one way to deal with the situation, namely, to collect all the data possible and then arrive at a conclusion with a cool head as if it were only a magazine puzzle being worked out. On the surface things looked mixed.

Item 1: Had I overshot Camooweal? For I imagined Camooweal in the centre of the boundless unvarying plains, like a raft in the middle of an ocean, secured by only two cords, representing the tracks to and from the town.

Item 2: Had I crossed this east-west track to Camooweal? Just imagine! one only has to look at the instrument board for ten seconds when flying at 100 feet in that haze, and zip! the track has slipped unnoticed beneath.

Item 3: Had I petrol enough to enable me to take the air again?

Depression began to set in, so much so that I could see I must get to work immediately before I became too firmly bogged in it.

But my limbs said " No! " and " No " it would have remained had not the buzz of a fly recalled to me the forgotten plague of those pests. I jumped up and went over to the plane for my map. This was the most urgent : to work out an estimate of my position before the details of last night's flight faded from my memory.

I spread the map on a tin while I sat on the boat and got busy with ruler, protractor, and compasses. Alexandra station 5.5 p.m. At 70 m.p.h. I would reach the water hole, where the track had disappeared at 5.57. I couldn't understand this for a

191

start. It had seemed only 30 instead of 52 minutes. But I must let it pass as there was no other water hole shown. Thence I had flown (with drift corrected) seven miles to the east, ten miles to the south, ten miles east, then on a course of 150⁰. After deducting a drift of 20⁰ this would result in a track of 130⁰, or practically S.E. I had continued on this track till a quarter to seven. So I marked on the map, seven miles east, then ten south, then ten east, then 32 S.E.

According to the resultant estimate of my position, Camooweal should be lying just ten miles to the east of where we were.

Now, petrol. The gauge showed empty. I shook the plane by one wing. There was an almost imperceptible movement at the empty mark. I could hear some splash in the tank. I would measure it. But not yet, no.

I fished out my hat, took a shirt, and buttoning it at the neck slipped it over the hat, leaving a small aperture of about two inches wide in front. It was rather difficult to see with this affair, but it kept most of the flies away. They disliked entering the shaded opening. I then made a circuit of the water hole and came to the following conclusions: The formed and metalled road about which I had been so excited must remain a mystery for the present; it petered out completely a hundred yards short of the water hole. There were no tracks on it and none issued from it, and so it could have no importance for me. From the east came a number of old tracks, motor car and big wagon, but when I hunted for a continuance of them on the west side it did not exist, and it became clear that they were only the tracks of vehicles that had come to, and stopped at, the water hole. There were a

192

number of tracks to the south and south-west, but investigation proved them to have been made by cattle seeking the water hole. The only thing at all cheering was the track of a shod horse which appeared to have passed within the last two or three days. However, as no other similar track was visible, it did not look as though the horseman made frequent visits. On the whole it was disappointing. I was returning to the shed when suddenly I spotted the tracks of a wagon; they were undoubtedly fresh. I got quite excited. I might have wondered why I had not seen them before, but my brain was not too brilliant; I turned and followed them gaily. My enthusiasm was short-lived. After fifty yards I found I was following the tracks of my own aeroplane.

I returned to the shed and had another long pull at the water tin. I wondered if I would silt up inside if I drank much more of the water without eating. I still found repellent the idea of eating anything. I made a thorough inspection of the sheds. By the side of the engine was a stack of benzine cases. I shook them one by one, only to find they were all empty. There was a full four-gallon tin of oil. This was as useful as a gold mine to a starving man. Of petrol there was not a sign. Two birds, crows or vultures I think, came and made harsh unpleasant noises on the trees near by. One fancied that they were jeering.

After taking another rest I decided that now at last the only thing that remained to be done was the measuring of the petrol. I had all the rest of the data. I took the tin in which the first lot of water had been boiled overnight, emptied out the residue of slime, swilled out the tin, wiped it dry with my handkerchief, then measured the height of the tin and divided it into four to represent gallons. I climbed on to the wing and held the tin underneath the petrol cock attached to the top centre section tank. Lord! how slowly it drained, and how my arm ached holding up the tin. I dared not fix it in any way. If it should slip and spill its contents! My muscles felt at breaking point before two gallons were drawn off. These I emptied into the back tank with infinite caution, begrudging even the evaporation that must have taken place. After a short spell I tried again. I was just beginning to warm with hope when it petered out. I checked up with a foot rule. There was exactly one gallon more. Total, three gallons.

Where possible I had always kept a careful record of, and check on, the petrol consumption. Except in bad weather it rarely varied from 4.9 to 5 gallons per hour. I would estimate at 5 g.p.h. Three gallons was therefore good for thirty-six minutes' flying.

I went back to the boat to work out the possibilities before me. With the tin of fat and my provisions I should be able to keep myself alive for at least a month; and if, during that time, having an axe and an air pistol, I could not devise some method of procuring food, I should not deserve to live. If I saved my petrol I had the means of taking to the air if I heard an aeroplane anywhere within, say, five miles. If I waited for another day I should get a rest, and some fresh idea might possibly occur to me during it. If I waited till the atmosphere cleared itself of sand and dust, my chances would be immeasurably increased. Instead of groping about near the earth with a visibility of a few hundred yards I should be able to see from ten to twenty miles in every direction. And once

I had used up my petrol—what a useless thing a plane would be! Obviously the reasonable course of action was to wait for the air to clear; that meant also rest, and again, the possibility of something turning up meanwhile.

But a day's delay would mean my incompetence being telegraphed all over the world. Search parties would be out. Someone might crash looking for me. I thought with shrinking of the publicity given to, and hard things said about another airman who had got recently into just such a predicament. I might that very moment be only a few miles from some place. I dreaded the idea of being searched for. No, I would give it a buck straight away. If I missed I should have to stay on the ground and wait. But the very fact of then having no petrol and therefore no other course open to me would be better than the thought that some human habitation might perhaps be lying quite near and within the range afforded by the petrol.

As for starvation in the event of not being found, and questions such as whether these millions of flies could not be turned into food at a pinch : these matters could be deferred till I had failed. Of my thirty-six minutes I would use three minutes to warm up the engine, then I would fly east for fifteen minutes, and if nothing turned up during that time I would use the other eighteen minutes to get myself back again to the water hole, where I thought I could at least keep alive.

I went and searched for the best place to get off from and land on again on returning, but taking everything into consideration I could not see anything better than the grass patch at the water hole. I set about packing everything up,

and an awful drag it was, too. But I took especial
care to wrap up the wine well. I thought of
leaving a note at the water hole to say I had been
there, but that seemed too cocksure, as if I thought
I should not have to return; so I did not tempt
Providence, and even left the boiled water in the
other tin all ready for my return.

I warmed up the engine. The three minutes
allotted to this operation seemed an age. Then I
took off for a flight as exciting during every second
of it as any I have ever experienced. There was
a strong wind blowing from the south, and the
dust haze was very thick. This time the minutes
fled as fast as they had travelled slowly the night
before. Five minutes went by. Not a sign of
anything. At nine minutes I crossed a fence and
I felt a momentary excitement which subsided
when I thought it might be one hundred miles from
anywhere. At eleven minutes I thought I saw a
man ahead. I strained my eyesight looking: it
turned out to be a small horse, which bolted when
I approached. At fourteen minutes and a half I
came to a creek. Well, I felt quite a sense of
relief. The question was settled for me. I had to
return and stay by the water hole, that was the
end of it! No more use reasoning, arguing, de-
bating. I decided to cross the creek and turn on
the other side. I was just going into the bank for
turning when I caught the dull glint of light on an
iron roof. I felt a jolt just as a horse might give
when it shies suddenly. An iron shed! Another
—five, six, seven of them. I thought: " I'm at
Avon Downs Station! " I outcursed and outswore
any trooper or bargee who ever lived. I set about
landing. The first shot I bumped and went off
again. I felt I didn't care two hoots in hades for

anything, and belted round the place at full throttle, all the better pleased the more petrol I used. The second attempt I was landing across the wind with a lot of drift and went off again.

The third time I got down all right. It was blowing pretty strongly, so I did not like to turn the machine to taxi towards the buildings. I sat tight and waited.

Presently the station book-keeper arrived in a truck loaded with blacks and station hands. I thought his Scotch accent was the pleasantest sound I had heard for a long time. Just as I shall never admire any scenery as much as I did those tin sheds. What they thought of me I can have no idea, for I blazed away with the most awful language a man could ever hear. I cussed myself, I cussed the Scottie, I cussed Elijah, I cussed everything I could think of cussing.

After that I began firing off questions by the dozen while they drove back to the station buildings :

(1) This was Rocklands Station. (2) Area, quite small, only 3,400 square miles. I thought they were a trifle modest about this, but they explained by comparing it with Alexandra near by, a station of 12,000 square miles. (3) The formed and metalled road was the work of a fire-plough. (4) The water hole was on Cattle Creek and probably would not have been visited for six weeks or until another drought set in necessitating the pumping of water. (5) Rocklands was four miles north of Camooweal; this meant that the water hole was about ten miles north of where I had thought it to be. This makes me think the bore where I missed the track must have been an extra one not shown on the map. (6) The water at the

197

bore ought to be quite healthy to drink. This I don't know about because I had dysentery for three weeks after. (7) All the other England to Sydney fliers had got bushed in the same locality.

Presently the manager, Mr. Little, arrived and took me along for some tea and something to eat. I could hardly stop talking long enough to drink the tea. I had had a scare and when, on arriving at Camooweal, they told me that a storm ahead had uprooted the telegraph line and made flying impossible, I used this as a pretext for going no farther. This day I had made my shortest run of nineteen miles. Short, and very very sweet.

CHAPTER XVI

CAMOOWEAL was a novelty to me. A few hotels, a few houses, and a hospital, all of tin, and situated in an open plain bearing a decided resemblance to a desert. As for the men, I understand Ludendorff to have said that after the crack British regiments, the Australian and New Zealand troops were the most formidable. And, by Jove, when you see these chaps in the back of Australia you can readily believe it.

But the Camoowealites are pretty touchy. For instance, the pain and woe caused by a certain lady flier over this route is still related. A banquet was prepared in her honour and the pilot's. On being approached as to the dish most calculated to catch her fancy, she replied that the joy of her life at that moment would be a little salad made of succulent green lettuce.

Alas! and alack! it had not rained for nine years, and the inhabitants, after biting off their finger-nails in pain and anguish, are said to have donned sackcloth and ashes.

My previous day's run had been 820 miles. With to-day's 19 my chance of doing the Darwin-Sydney run in three days vanished completely, so I decided to jog along quietly.

I had borrowed four gallons of petrol from Mr.

199

Little, and at Camooweal re-filled with 54 gallons more. Next morning we got away at 6.30.

I had been advised that the weather was very bad at Cloncurry, 170 miles beyond Camooweal. But it was not till McKinlay, 80 miles the far side of Cloncurry, that we ran into rain. When I first caught sight of the rain-clouds ahead, having the monsoons fresh in my memory, the thought of more trouncing was most disagreeable. However, when we got into it, it seemed nothing in comparison. It was a great relief to find it no worse. From now on, the whole country was saturated with water, and vast stretches of it in the grips of a flood were entirely inundated. The only disadvantage about it for me was the cold resulting from my getting wet, and the knowledge that Elijah would need a new nose if I had to land on the saturated ground.

It was amusing to see a troop of horses bolting at the sound of the aeroplane above them. It was all they could do to draw their feet out of the mud, leaving a small well behind at each step. You could see their whole bodies leaning forward to give them the power to overcome the suction.

At Winton, at the 380 mile peg, we came across a railway line not charted on either of the maps I was carrying. However, as it pointed in the direction I wanted to follow, I came to the conclusion it must be going to Longreach, so stuck to it. It was a terribly boring trip, all the country being very monotonous. It rained pretty hard the whole way, but worst of all we had a strong head wind against us, and the whole day's journey only averaged 60 miles an hour. In an aeroplane this is deadly.

On arriving at Longreach I found strips of

metal a few yards wide laid down on the aerodrome. There were three strips, making the shape
of a triangle. The idea is to land on the most
suitable of these strips when the rest of the aerodrome is a bog, as it was then. Mr. Baird, of
Quantas Air Service, waved me to land on one
strip which would have necessitated a cross wind
landing. I had one shot, thinking the other strips
must be out of use, but I was drifting too much,
so went off again. Next shot I made a rotten
landing on another strip. Nothing is so calculated
to make you land badly as 8¾ hours' flying in bad
weather at 60 miles an hour. At the end of the
run Elijah ran one wheel into the mud, and was
immediately pulled up with a jerk. Fortunately
she did not go over on her nose, so all was well.
Although the run was only 552 miles, it was as
dreary as any I can think of.

I spent a very interesting evening with Mr.
Baird and some others. Mr. Baird is the man who
builds the D.H. 50's for Quantas Air Service.

Next morning we left Longreach at 7.48 and
reached Charleville, after an easy run, at 11.40.
The only event was spotting a kangaroo in the
middle of a vast flat plain. I was so interested that I
turned and swooped within a few feet of his head.
It never moved, but just stood looking at me in a
stupid way, flopping its front paws about in the air.
After I had passed I saw it lolloping away slowly
like a very hay-seedy farm labourer going to work.

I never saw such an enthusiastic place as Charle-
ville. The whole town had turned out, which made
me as nervous as the deuce in landing. Then the
Mayor and Town Council held a reception in the
Town Hall, complete with beer and lemonade.
After that I found Mr. Smith, manager of the

Petrol Company for Brisbane, had flown over that morning from Brisbane, and arranged a luncheon of some fifty people in my honour.

I have often been asked what was the worst moment of the flight, and I think this was it, when I was called on to try and make a speech.

After the luncheon party, which I would have enjoyed even more if I had not had the thought of a good bit of a day's work yet to be done, I took off again at three o'clock. I was astounded at the warmness of the welcome they had given me at Charleville, and left feeling very nervous about what the future was going to hold, considering that Charleville is not a very big place; but I think an airman gets a bigger ration of welcome per head of population from Charleville than from any other place in the world. Only, if I may say so, judging by the names scribbled on my aeroplane, I think it is doubtful if any of the schoolboys there could win a handwriting competition.

I landed at Bourke, 3 hours and 35 minutes later, to find another welcome waiting for me. This day I had flown for 7 hours and 27 minutes, covered 552 miles, been to a hefty luncheon party in the middle of the day, and a pretty solid dinner at the end of it. Life was getting strenuous.

On getting out to the aerodrome next morning there was a red dust storm blowing, which prevented me seeing more than 50 to 100 yards ahead. However, I presumed it would be all right once I was above it, so I taxied to the end of the aerodrome, with two chaps hanging on to each wing, and took off. As soon as we got above the storm the air was quite clear. I rid my eyes, nose, mouth and ears of the greater part of the accumulated red dust, and after that the run to Narromine was

202

quite easy. Here I came down for a cup of tea at the invitation of the Narromine Aero Club. This must be one of the smallest clubs in the world, for when I asked how many planes they had, the reply was " None."

Soon after leaving this town the flat seemingly endless plains at last broke up, and soon we were traversing the Blue Mountains, a very pleasant but uneventful flight. The N.S.W. Aero Club had asked me to rendezvous at Sydney Harbour Bridge at three o'clock, at the height of 4,000 feet, where an escort of ten planes was to pick me up. Approaching Sydney I tried really for the first time to sum up the performance I had put up :

1. I had not beaten Hinkler's record.

2. I had not done what I had really wanted even more, namely, to fly solo half-way round the earth. To do this is exceedingly difficult without crossing the Atlantic or Pacific. In fact, I do not think it has ever yet been done even in a big machine, except that Kingsford-Smith would have had he flown to Spain instead of England. This is just as good of course. Apart from this flight I do not think the flights claimed to have been made round the world, or half round the world, can be truthfully said to have been so. To fly round the world you must pass through the antipodes of your starting point. If this is not so, where is the line to be drawn with such flights? Has a man who flies round the North Pole also flown round the world?

I think flying from Spain to New Zealand is the only way a true flight half-way round the world can be made without crossing the Atlantic or Pacific.

When I started I had intended having a shot at

203

the Tasman. I thought I could fluke it with the aid of another 40-gallon tank of petrol. I had always believed the distance to be 1,235 miles; but at Tripoli, when I went into the matter thoroughly, I discovered to my horror that this distance was in sea miles and that the real distance was about 1,450 miles. This it would be folly to attempt in such a machine.

3. Even in my attempt to cross Australia in three days I had failed. The best I could claim was the 12,655 miles between Tripoli and Sydney, which took me 22 days. An average of about 575 miles a day for the 22 days. Hinkler averaged 760 miles a day for 16 days. And it is just the higher average which counts. The merit of this flight is only to be judged by the time taken to carry it out. If it were undertaken by easy short stages in good weather the flight would present no difficulty. In fact, given the time, it would be easy to fly anywhere in the world overland. It is interesting to look at Lindberg's flight—the dandy of solos—in this light as one of 3,200 miles in two days, or 1,600 miles a day for two days.

The nearer we got to Sydney the more depressed I became. I was a human 22-day clock beginning to run down. After being wound up at Tripoli I had been ticking away every day from before dawn till frequently an hour or two after sunset. It had become a habit. And now the clock was just about to stop, to leave a desolation, an emptiness, a solitariness in place of its steady tick.

But by this time I had reached the suburbs of Sydney and excitement chased out all other sensations. I recalled the only other time I had visited the city, crawling into the harbour in a dirty, boring old tub of a boat. Lor! I should soon

APPROACHING MASCOT AERODROME

Facing page 204

again be a slave to petty circumstances and petty officials. In the air . . . . well, one was a slave there as much, if not more so, than anywhere else. Yet how much grander the masters to serve: Father Time, as usual; Aurora, the goddess of dawn; Vesper, the goddess of night; Jupiter, the god of thunder (weather); and lastly, Minerva.

On arrival at the bridge I was twenty minutes or so late and found no one there, until a Ryan monoplane came into sight. A photographer pointed a huge camera and took several shots of old Elijah. As nobody else turned up, and I did not know the position of Mascot aerodrome, I decided to stick to the Ryan, which presently led me to it. When it came into sight, I could see planes leaving the ground in a stream. As they began to fly round me, I got more and more nervous. After flying round like a flock of disturbed seagulls the planes all landed one after another. Then came my turn. I was far more nervous than if I had been making a forced landing. However, I determined this should be a beauty for once, having spotted several thousand people watching down below. I did an approach to get my eye in, as a golfer swings his club, and next time came in all ready for a super-perfect landing. First of all I bumped hard, then, shooting up into the air, I was landing perfectly all right when I realised just in time that it was ten feet above the ground, whereupon I felt quite grateful for being able to fake it into a very ordinary rabbit-hop finish.

Ensued for me a turmoil. The tremendous hospitality of the Australians and of the New Zealanders in Sydney, being interviewed by reporters, answering cables from all over the world, answering letters, answering calls, answering 'phone calls. The N.S.W. Aero Club, the largest in the world, gave a dance for me and made me an honorary life member of the Club—an honour I very greatly appreciated, for are not the Australian pilots among the best in the world? There was something on all day and every day. It is quite impossible to enumerate the hundreds of instances of hospitality, friendliness and kindness shown me; my ambition was to show how I appreciated every one of them, in spite of the fact that life for me had now ceased to be worth living. I still had dysentery besides complete nervous exhaustion. I had done roughly 352 hours' work in three weeks and a day, but I do not think the exhaustion was caused so much by this as by the agoraphobia, fear of crowds and strangers, from which I began to suffer. And every night almost without fail for nine weeks I had the same nightmare between three and four o'clock. I was in the air flying when my vision went completely and I waited in fearful darkness for the inevitable crash. Usually I woke to find myself clawing at the window or a wall, trying to escape.

There were one or two relieving incidents. A reception by the Mayor and Councillors of Mascot borough, when everyone in the room made a speech and beer was mixed (sometimes) with lemonade, recalled the reception by the same company to Moir and Owen. These airmen, it will be remembered, had flown out from England in a Vickers Vimy and had the misfortune to crash in the dark into the potato patch of a lighthouse-keeper near Darwin. At the reception given them, which began at two o'clock in the Town Hall, some 14 or 15 speeches were made in their honour. Everything was going splendidly, when at about 4.30 somebody suddenly had a bright idea, and the question was put: "Where *are* Moir and Owen?" The more they searched, the more apparent it became that Messrs. Moir and Owen were not present. (Sensation.) The missing airmen were discovered sitting huddled up in a car just outside the Town Hall, and shivering in the drizzling rain.

There was another incident which I thought rather good: a newspaper, the "Sydney Sun," telegraphing offers of £15 15s. for an exclusive story of the flight. After spending roughly £3,000 on the preparations for and the carrying out of it, I did not feel inclined to commercialise it even for such a fine journalistic reward.

Flying is the most fascinating sport in the world; it enters ineradicably into your blood. Personally I find myself planning within a month of finishing this flight how I can make and save enough money to try another. That feeling of cutting out big distances in an apparatus controlled and directed by yourself alone; the attempt by you, a solitary soul from among two thousand millions, to do something that no other of the 1,999,999,999 has done tickles your vanity, your sense of power, your sense of romance, your love of excitement, as nothing else in the world can do.

And so there was a crash and the red wine trickled and dripped off the propeller boss, spilled for the honour of Minerva, a goddess.

SOLO TO SYDNEY

Actual Time Taken on Journey

	Time	Distances Miles	Non-stop runs exceeding 500 miles
London-Pisa	11.50	866	534
Pisa-Tripoli	14.05	1040	629
Tripoli-Benghazi	6.12	612	612
Benghazi-Abu-Sueir	9.15	854	854 n.s.
Abu-Sueir-Rutba Wells ...	6.43	582	none
Rutba Wells-Bushire	8.43	828	574
Bushire-Chahbar	9	760	560
Chahbar-Karachi	6.05	430	none
Karachi-Jhansi	8.40	761	516
Jhansi-Calcutta	7.05	687	none
Calcutta-Rangoon	8.45	770	none
Rangoon-Victoria Point ...	7.45	610	610
Victoria Point-Singapore...	10.00	779	779
Singapore-Batavia	8.38	660	660
Batavia-Sourabaja	6.25	424	none
Sourabaja-Bima	5.55	460	none
Bima-Atemboea	6.45	510	510
Atemboea-Darwin	6.10	512	512
Darwin-Waterhole	11.20	820	640
Waterhole-Camooweal ...	19½	19	none
Camooweal-Longreach ...	8.48	552	552
Longreach-Bourke	7.27	570	none
Bourke-Sydney	6.35	455	none
	182.30½	14,561	